'David explains beautifully, in his calming and clear way, how everything I fully believe to be true actually is. He has a way of putting facts into fiction and science into soul food. I use his workings daily to bring backbone and clarification to my own inner musings and beliefs. This book is another must-read if self-growth is your bag.'

DONNA ASHWORTH, *SUNDAY TIMES* BEST-SELLING AUTHOR OF
I WISH I KNEW

'I love David's work, particularly his ongoing campaign to centre kindness as a core societal value, and to elevate its practice to that of a daily tool which has the potential to radically transform the health of our communities. This book teaches that while the effort to drop our defensive postures and choose to be kind is not always easy or straightforward, it doesn't need to be grand or awe-inspiring to have a great impact. David reminds us that the power of caring lies in its humility and simplicity, which each and every one of us can harness to enjoy the good days and get through the tough ones together.'

EVANNA LYNCH, ACTRESS AND AUTHOR OF
THE OPPOSITE OF BUTTERFLY HUNTING

'Imagine if nine billion people performed one act of kindness a day. We would create a climate change from fear to love in no time at all. The world would be changed and so would you. *The Joy of Actually Giving a F*ck* is a masterful, how-to guide to help you 'go kindly' and make a real difference in the world.'

ROBERT HOLDEN, *NEW YORK TIMES* BEST-SELLING AUTHOR OF
SHIFT HAPPENS! AND *HIGHER PURPOSE*

'Dr. David Hamilton is a shining light in the world of wellness. His scientific approach yet accessible language mean everyone can benefit from his words in their life. Buy this book for everyone you love.'

DR. GEMMA NEWMAN, AUTHOR OF *GET WELL, STAY WELL*

'Kindness is essential for our collective well-being and David's practical advice mixed with hard-core science is the perfect blend to inspire more of it! The world needs this book.'

'A brilliant reflection on how every one of us has the capacity to improve our lives, by taking the responsibility to work on ourselves with all the challenges life brings with it, to be strong and kind with ourselves and the ones around us. David's ability to line out what we all know in our hearts to be true is second to none: That real trust and respect, supported by small genuine acts, make a huge difference in our personal and professional lives, with one caveat – you really have to mean it. A must-read for any leader who has the courage and strength to embark on a journey to create a competitive business with all the difficult choices that come with it, but is always committed to do it with genuine kindness and respect for their people.'

Also by David R. Hamilton

Books

Why Woo-Woo Works (2021)

The Little Book of Kindness (2019)

How Your Mind Can Heal Your Body (2008, 2018)

The Five Side Effects of Kindness (2017)

I Heart Me (2015)

Choice Point (2012)

Is Your Life Mapped Out? (2012)

The Contagious Power of Thinking (2011)

Why Kindness Is Good for You (2010)

Destiny Vs Free Will (2007)

It's the Thought That Counts (2006)

Audio teaching available on the *Empower You Unlimited Audio* app

Why Kindness Is Good for You

Why Gratitude Is Good for You

Why Meditation Is Good for You

How to Deflect Negative Emotion

Achieve Your Goals with Visualization

Learn to Love the Way You Look

The Mind–Body Connection

Heal Your Immune System with the Power of Thought

And more...

THE JOY OF ACTUALLY GIVING A F☺CK

David R. Hamilton Ph.D.

How kindness can cure stress and make you happy

HAY HOUSE

Carlsbad, California • New York City
London • Sydney • New Delhi

Published in the United Kingdom by:
Hay House UK Ltd, The Sixth Floor, Watson House,
54 Baker Street, London W1U 7BU
Tel: +44 (0)20 3927 7290; www.hayhouse.co.uk

Published in the United States of America by:
Hay House LLC, PO Box 5100, Carlsbad, CA 92018-5100
Tel: (1) 760 431 7695 or (800) 654 5126; www.hayhouse.com

Published in Australia by:
Hay House Australia Publishing Pty Ltd,
18/36 Ralph St, Alexandria NSW 2015
Tel: (61) 2 9669 4299; www.hayhouse.com.au

Published in India by:
Hay House Publishers (India) Pvt Ltd, Muskaan Complex,
Plot No.3, B-2, Vasant Kunj, New Delhi 110 070
Tel: (91) 11 4176 1620; www.hayhouse.co.in

Text © David R. Hamilton, 2024

The moral rights of the author have been asserted.

The information given in this book should not be treated as a substitute for professional medical advice; always consult a medical practitioner. Any use of information in this book is at the reader's discretion and risk. Neither the author nor the publisher can be held responsible for any loss, claim or damage arising out of the use, or misuse, of the suggestions made, the failure to take medical advice or for any material on third-party websites.

A catalogue record for this book is available from the British Library.

Tradepaper ISBN: 978-1-4019-7668-2
E-book ISBN: 978-1-83782-243-0
Audiobook ISBN: 978-1-83782-268-3

10 9 8 7 6 5 4 3 2 1

Printed in the United States of America

This product uses responsibly sourced papers and/or recycled materials. For more information, see www.hayhouse.com.

To my dad, Robert Hamilton
1943–2022

Contents

Introduction   xi

1. Kindfulness   1

2. How mindfulness can make you selfish   25

3. A superfood for your mental health   47

4. The opposite of stress   75

5. Most heroes don't wear capes   89

6. Mindfully kind   107

7. Why you should be kind to yourself   139

8. Lead with kindness   175

9. Kindness conundrums   191

10. Kindness isn't always clear-cut   217

Appendix I: The seven-day kindness challenge   237
Appendix II: Kindfulness meditation practices   239
Notes   245
Acknowledgments   253
About the Author   255

Introduction

Why should you give a f*ck? And what should you be giving a f*ck about? Age-old questions.

Buddha asked the same ones, only in the language of the day. In the annals of time, no one ever wrote a song about the virtues of being an ass. But kindness? It's been the star of tales, poems, songs, and stories since forever.

For starters, it's the right thing to do. Remember that time you complimented your friend's new haircut? Boom! You just added a sprinkle of glitter to their day. Kindness has this magical power to turn gray skies into unicorn rainbows, one compliment at a time.

Kindness is the stitching in the fabric of life. It's the spice in friendship soup. Without it, we're all just walking around with our separate pieces of cloth or holding our own spices. Let's face it, the world needs people who help other people. It brings us all together in life's big recipe.

Because some people are having a tough time. You might be one of them. So let's give a f*ck about each other and see what happens. Let's try not to be too hard on people, as you never know what they're going through. Trade those put-downs for some 'keep going' cheer.

And, boy, does kindness feels good! Why? Because it plays around with your brain chemistry in some interesting ways and serves you up some hefty doses of happy hormones. It's good for your heart and immune system. It can even reduce wrinkles. Yes, you heard that right. There's science that shows exactly how it works.

Who needs Botox when you can offer a friend a few kind words, hold some doors open, or let people in front of you in traffic with a smile? The secret is to mean it!

Being genuine with your kindness earns you something like Nature's karma points. It's like a secret high five from Nature because you're a superstar of civility. But if you're not genuine, well, Nature knows the difference. No high five.

Let's also think about the ripple effect. You hold a door for someone, they smile, and then they hold the elevator for someone else, and that person later buys a coffee for a friend. It's like a game of 'pay it forward,' but with coffee and heart-warming moments. And the crucial thing: You held a door, but someone you've never met got a free coffee out of it. That's got to be cool. That's how life works. These ripple effects are everywhere.

Now, I'm not saying you have to start hugging every cactus in sight, but being kind is like giving a cozy blanket to your and everyone else's soul on a cold winter's day. It's the ultimate cheat code for turning frowns upside down, with a side of happy dances.

Let's not forget to give a f*ck about ourselves too. If you're always pouring love and kindness into others but forget to fill up your own cup, you'll end up running on fumes. And who wants that?

Being kind to yourself involves hitting the pause button when you need a rest, saying 'no, thanks' when you're already juggling enough, and cheering yourself on when things get a bit chaotic (because, let's face it, we're only human).

The skill with self-kindness is in finding the balance, that sweet spot between kindness to others while also being kind to yourself. Later in this book, I'll show you a heap of ways you can be kind to yourself.

I also tackle the complicated bits about kindness. Because kindness isn't always clear-cut. Sometimes when you're kind to one person, another person will accuse you of not being kind to them. We've all been there. Just who should you be dishing out your doses of kindness to? And how do you know what the right thing is? We'll be tackling that minefield and a few other kindness conundrums later in the book.

There you have it - kindness, the unsung hero of the human experience. It's like chocolate for the heart, a good hair day for the soul, and a virtual high five for humanity.

So go forth, be a valiant kindness crusader, and spread those warm and fuzzy vibes like confetti at a unicorn parade.

Kindfulness

Have you ever wondered why the world seems to be so chaotic, complicated, and downright crabby sometimes? One reason might be that we've forgotten how important it is to genuinely give a f*ck about each other. Here's why that matters.

For starters, kindness feels good! Remember the last time someone held the door for you, smiled at you randomly, or just listened when you had a really crappy day? Felt nice, right?

That's because kindness is like this universal language that, deep down, we all understand and appreciate. Plus, as we'll see, it sets off a feel-good party in our brain and heart that actually makes us happier and reduces our blood pressure.

Life's a team sport. Like it or not, we're all on this giant rock called Earth together. It's a group project, and we all know that group projects suck when one person is slacking off or being an ass. When we support each other, life gets a little easier and a lot more fun.

And you know what? Karma's a thing. Forget the mystical side of it for a second. Let's think practically. If you help out today, there's a good chance someone will be there for you tomorrow. Call it 'selfish altruism' if you will, but it works! Being an ass usually comes back to bite you on the rear end.

Let's not forget human connection. Believe it or not, our brains are hardwired to connect. That's right: Every like, share, comment, hug, or chat over coffee is more than just a moment – it's our brain's way of saying, 'Hey, I need this to feel alive and happy.' So why starve it?

Giving a f*ck about each other makes the world less scary. The more we care about others, the more we realize that most people are just like us – trying to figure things out and hoping for a good day. It's easier to fear what you don't know, but once you get to know people, the world seems a lot smaller and cozier.

So next time you're tempted to scroll past someone's problem, dismiss someone's feelings, or just be in your own little bubble, remember: The world's a better place when we all give a little f*ck. Let's sprinkle that stuff everywhere like it's magical kindness glitter!

Now, this first chapter is called 'Kindfulness.' Sounds like mindfulness, doesn't it? That's not an accident.

Once upon a time, mindfulness was mostly about being mindfully aware as part of doing other stuff and that often meant being kind. It still does to some people, mostly mindfulness teachers.

But in the ever-evolving quest for inner peace and mental well-being that we're all on and that's become so fashionable these days, mindfulness meditation has emerged as a cornerstone practice. It's rooted in ancient wisdom and fortified by contemporary psychology. It says, 'be present,' 'observe your thoughts without judgment,' and 'cultivate an awareness of the now.'

The trouble is, most people nowadays learn it from an app. While I love apps, they need to grab our attention early on. So you open the app, the instruction is usually short and then – boom! – you know mindfulness. It's like a scene from *The Matrix*, where Neo receives a download and then reports, 'I know kung fu.'

But the original teaching of mindfulness came from Buddhism and was much more extensive. It included instruction on ethics; that is, in kind and compassionate thinking, attitudes, how to communicate without being a grump, and moral conduct. It was the full-course meal – ethics, kindness, and good vibes all rolled into one.

Fast forward to the 1980s and 1990s, and to make the practice more acceptable in clinical environments, mindfulness sought a divorce from its ethical roots. It was a trial separation at first.

It was remixed into mindfulness-based stress reduction (MBSR), which was designed to reduce stress and improve psychological well-being in hospital outpatients. It was *mindfulness light*, minus all the ethical, cultural, and kindness-based teachings.

And, wow, did the light version hit the big leagues! Schools, tech giants like Google, even the US Army were all over it. It was mindfulness without the strings attached. Forget about the deep soulful stuff; just sit, breathe, and voilà!

It was all about the psychological benefits of the seated practice and how they could benefit the individual and the organization. The divorce was finalized, the papers signed. There was no going back.

Now, with our tech skyrocketing faster than you can say 'namaste,' mindfulness has had the app treatment. But just remember, while apps might make things snappy, sometimes you're just swiping left on the real essence. There's more to mindfulness than a digital quickie.

Why should you give a f*ck anyway if mindfulness is now mindfulness light? If it works for you then great, awesome. Case closed.

But it's not just about you – it's about *us*. Like it or not, we're in this game called Life together and the sooner we start helping each other, the easier it's going to be to get to the next level. Expanding your view from 'me' to 'us' can really ramp up the positive vibes flying around and dish out a whole load of health benefits for you and your loved ones that you wouldn't even imagine. But I'll move on to that soon. I'm getting a bit ahead of myself here. Back to mindfulness.

Nowadays, hardly anyone who learns mindfulness knows how it was originally taught, and the importance that was placed upon kindness in how we think, speak, and act.

Maybe it's time for mindfulness to get back into bed with kindness.

Where did mindfulness come from?

The Axial Age is a historical period between the 8th and 3rd centuries BCE, first identified by the German psychiatrist and philosopher Karl Jaspers in his book *The Origin and Goal of History*. It's fascinating, because during this time there was a big shift in religious and philosophical thought in loads of places around the world. This happened in tandem in Persia, India, China, the Levant (Eastern Mediterranean and Western Asia, covering the Middle East), and throughout the Greco-Roman world – and there wasn't any seeming chat between them.

Almost as if by magic, several big-time thinkers emerged. They're household names now. In the centuries that followed, their words would go on to define whole tracks of religious and philosophical thought. Take a bow, Confucius, Zarathustra (Zoroaster), Homer, Plato, and Buddha.

According to legend, the Buddha started life as royalty. Prince Siddhartha, fed up with having everything he wanted handed to him, wished to see what life was really like. In the dead of night, he left the palace that was his home to spend the next several years as a pauper on the streets, witnessing the kind of poverty and hardship that had been kept from him all his life.

To cut a long story short, he eventually figured out the nature of suffering; basically, everyone suffers and there are common causes. He identified solutions to suffering that were easy for people to practice. The story goes that he became enlightened while sitting under the Bodhi tree and was later given the title 'Buddha.'

Some of his solutions are found in the Eightfold Path. It's here that the Buddha teaches mindfulness.

But it's not exactly mindfulness as we know it today. Mindfulness as we think of it in the West is known by Buddhist scholars as *contemporary* (or modern) mindfulness, or sometimes secular mindfulness, as it's without any connection with religion. The original teaching of Buddha's is known as *traditional* mindfulness.

In a nutshell, the main difference between them is that traditional mindfulness is grounded in a set of teachings around being a decent person and refraining from hurting people.

That set of teachings is called the Eightfold Path. It served as a kind of training manual, helping practitioners orient their moral compass and guiding them in how to reduce suffering and be a fairly upstanding citizen in the process. The practical mindfulness meditation technique that we all know about today was a small step on the path.

The Eightfold Path

Here follows a wee summary of the Eightfold Path so you can see for yourself. Now, I'm not a Buddhist and entire books have been written about this that are hundreds of pages long, so take my summary lightly. It's just to give you an idea of where mindfulness was first placed.

1. Right view

Stuff changes all the time! It's called *impermanence*. By accepting this, we stop trying to cling to things as if they were our favorite bar of chocolate. There's also a common-sense element to right view. Basically, good actions = good results, while bad actions = 'why did I do that?' moments.

2. Right intention

Cultivate a kind mind. Don't just *be* kind, but think kindly of people too. Kindness starts in your own head by thinking kind thoughts – just as you'd prefer it if people thought kindly about you and looked past all your 'ahem' moments. And if a thought doesn't spark joy, be aware of it and let it go. No need for the negativity baggage.

3. Right speech

Chat responsibly. If you don't have anything nice to say, then don't say anything at all. If it's not nice, true, or necessary, zip it. And there's definitely no room for gossip, rumors, or mean comments. Words are superpowers, use them for good!

4. Right action

This is like your moral GPS. Are you acting from a place of compassion or kindness? Great, then proceed. If not, it's time to reroute. And this includes general life advice: Don't steal. Don't kill.

5. Right livelihood

Basically, don't take up a job that goes against being a good human. If it hurts others, it's a no-go.

6. Right effort

Think of this as going to the 'gym for your soul.' Flex muscles of kindness and mindfulness. It's not about grinding hard, but more about the steady, feel-good burn.

7. Right mindfulness

Live in the moment – not in the last episode of that show you watched on Netflix or in what's for dinner or even that conversation you had this afternoon. It's about being right here, right now.

8. Right concentration

This is like the Zen mode on your phone but for your mind. Find your focus, get into the groove, and the other seven steps become a walk in the park!

There you have it. The Eightfold Path: your comprehensive guide to being a chilled, mindfully kind human being. Mindfully kind. Not just mindful. It says don't hurt people. Be kind in how you think, speak, and act.

So, you can see where mindfulness came from, and that it was more than a meditation practice, but also a lot about being mindfully kind. That's why I like the word 'kindfulness.' Mindfully kind. Mindfulness with a sprinkle of kindness. Have a kind mind. Give a shit about people. If someone's having a tough time, offer them a hug, lend them a sympathetic ear, buy them a coffee. Just be kind, however it looks. Don't be an asshole. The end.

Mindfulness was taught alongside the other steps because it meant that as you grow to become all Zen and wisdomous (I know that's not a real word but I'm a fan of the sitcom *Friends*, and it's one of my favorite ever words that Joey used), the new and improved You would be of benefit to everybody. We're in this thing, life, together, and with you becoming a better person and all, it's good for each and every one of us. It orients your moral compass away from your own self-interest in a direction that's better for everyone – your family, your friends, your colleagues, even that person who serves you in the store who never smiles.

The focus of contemporary mindfulness, on the other hand, is to benefit the individual. Let me be clear, though. This isn't in a selfish way, but to help us to better manage our emotions and deal with stress in our modern world. And let's face it, we need that help in a world that seems to be spinning faster and faster. It's a great tool, a therapy that helps us cope with the challenges of modern living.

Where contemporary mindfulness is more about the *me* in meditation, traditional mindfulness, like kindfulness, is about all of us.

What caused the divorce?

I mentioned earlier how mindfulness sought a divorce from its ethical roots. It wasn't a falling out or anything like that. It's just that most clinical settings in the West are secular. You can't be professing morals or ethics when there could sometimes be psychologically vulnerable people around, no matter how well intentioned. It's science over sermons, so to speak!

So when mindfulness made its debut in the West, it had to don a lab coat and specs. It needed to be in a form that could be tested and be shown that it could deliver clear clinical benefits to people. Otherwise, no one would have listened. This was downtown Boston, after all, not a monastery in Tibet.

Jon Kabat-Zinn was instrumental. He took up meditation when he was a student at MIT. By 1971 he had a Ph.D. in molecular biology and accepted a job as a faculty member at Brandeis University, where he taught molecular genetics and a general science course for non-science majors. Then, during a two-week Vipassana retreat (an intense meditation practice where you meditate for several hours a day), he had an 'aha' moment – how to bring mindfulness to the West.

He appreciated that while the benefits of meditation could be life-changing, the language and cultural accompaniment wouldn't catch on with Westerners. It had to be slimmed down. Chill without the spiritual extras, so it would appeal to the people who needed it most, people who were suffering and needed some relief.

He was working in a hospital at the time, so he figured it would be the ideal place to try out a streamlined mindfulness. In the spring of 1979, he met individually with the clinical directors of the primary care, pain, and orthopedic clinics at the hospital. Would they be open to referring patients to his program? These would be patients who weren't responding to treatment, those they weren't able to help and who were, in effect, falling through the cracks in the healthcare system.

His course would be an eight-week stress-busting program for hospital outpatients. He wasn't saying 'forget the meds' but more like 'why not add this to the mix?' If it works, great. If it doesn't, patients would still be on their meds. No loss. It was like a 'try-before-you-buy' pitch to the hospital. So it began in the fall of 1979, when the first few cycles of patients were referred – and it was a hit.

Patients loved it and made significant improvements. Kabat-Zinn and the clinical directors were high-fiving its success. Word quickly spread further into the medical community and within a year, the chief of medicine invited Kabat-Zinn to make the course an official part of the department of medicine at the hospital.

And so it was that mindfulness had officially made it into the mainstream. Kabat-Zinn's genius had made mindfulness seem normal... without the bells and incense.

We know the program today as MBSR – mindfulness-based stress reduction – but that wasn't the name it started out with. There was no mention of mindfulness at all at first. Kabat-Zinn did his utmost to speak about it in ways that didn't sound 'mystical, New Age, or well, just plain flakey.' His words!

So it was christened the *Stress Reduction and Relaxation Program*. But after a few years of it running in the hospital, it morphed into the *Stress Reduction Clinic*. It was a clinical service in the department of medicine after all.

As there were other stress reduction programs around, as well as other meditation teachings in the USA at the time, in the 1990s it finally became known as MBSR to distinguish itself from these. Today, millions of people around the globe have MBSR to thank for some of their peaceful moments. There's now even a whole 'mindfulness family' with acronyms like MBRP, MBCP, and even MB-EAT. Yes, mindfulness-based eating. Zen while you dine.

But seriously, MBSR has helped millions of people around the world, not just in reducing stress and helping improve their mental health, but in many other ways too. Never heard of it? Don't worry, most people haven't. Because nowadays, it's all about quick and easy mindfulness via apps and books. A long explanation of the roots, basis, meaning, and context behind it would put most people off, especially in our modern day where everyone is competing for a slice of our attention.

Mindfulness 101

OK, before we go any further, you might have tried mindfulness before. Heck, you might even be an expert. But if you've never tried it, think of this as Mindfulness 101. If you have, think of it as a refresher.

First step? Breathe!

Yep, simple as that.

Feel it in your nose, tummy, or anywhere else your attention is drawn. Listen to it.

Thoughts will pop up. That's what thoughts do. No worries – think of them like balloons and let them float away.

If you catch your mind racing like a runaway train, where you're now having an imaginary argument with someone, same rule applies. Stand back, notice the thought, don't chase after it, don't judge it, then wave goodbye and refocus on your breathing.

There's magic in this: The moment you notice you're thinking, you stop thinking. You can't do both at the same time. Think or notice that you're thinking. It's always one or the other. If you notice that you're thinking, you'll stop thinking. And your mind will fall still.

This is mindfulness. Nonjudgmental awareness.

It's like mental gym time. It builds your mental muscles to help you fight off stress, flex a bit of resilience, and make lemonade when life is chucking lemons at you. With practice, it's a proper workout for your brain. And the brain-gains are real! (More on that later.)

If you've ever taken a proper eight-week-or-so mindfulness course, you'll learn that it's not all about the meditation practice. It's also about bringing mindfulness – awareness – to the moments of your daily life. That's what Kabat-Zinn taught as part of MBSR, long before it became mindfulness light.

It's about learning to live without just reacting to stuff or going through the motions. *Mindful* living rather than *mindless* living.

Mindful or mindless

The opposite of mindfulness is mindlessness, where you're so in your head that you barely notice anything. Sound like anyone you know? Yourself, perhaps? Maybe someone could dollop a whole tub of ice cream onto your shoes and you'd just glance up and smile politely before getting back to that all-important train of thought you're on. The problem is, while mindfulness helps us reduce stress, mindlessness *creates* it. Without the skill of stepping back nonjudgmentally, we may overreact to everything and make mountains out of molehills, or simply not pay attention to anything at all.

I do it too. I live close to the countryside, yet sometimes when I'm out walking, I forget to notice the beautiful scenery around me. The place is awash with green and color. Bushy trees, flowers, the scent of fresh air, birdsong everywhere. Nope. I might as well be walking along a gray corridor adorned with the odd metal radiator.

I'm in my head, going over a conversation I recently had, or one I need to have, or obsessing about how to write that book chapter a wee bit better. And getting stressed as a consequence.

Some of the stress comes from the mind going everywhere, and some comes from the effect that has on breathing. Being mindful calms your breathing because you're slowing your mind and taking your time, while mindlessness makes the breath short and shallow.

Most of us live our lives mindlessly. Yes, there are pockets of mindfulness, of course, but for the most part we're mindless.

I don't mean that we wander around like robotic automatons, but that we get constantly caught up in the daily grind and dramas of life without taking a step back to survey what's happening right under our noses, or to survey what's going on in our minds.

Mindfulness can help you take a step back – in your head. And that's where it matters.

We start to recognize that how we feel at any one time is a consequence not just of what seems to be happening in our lives, but of how we are *thinking* about what's happening in our lives. We learn to adjust how we feel by shifting our attention.

That's not to pretend that shit isn't happening at times when it clearly is. Not at all! Feelings are like a leaf blowing in the wind, but when you take more control of your mind, you can learn to hold that pesky leaf in the palm of your hand and guide it wherever you want it to be.

That's mindfulness. And it gets easier with practice.

At first you might last a few seconds and then your mind is away again. But in time and with practice, you can take hold of the leaf again and again and set it down on the table beside the flowers.

Why do people meditate?

The nastiest email I ever received was from a spiritual teacher. At the time it put me off ever wanting to be 'spiritual.' If that's what spiritual training does for you then I wanted none of it.

Most of the spiritual people I knew at that time were just ordinary folks with a select set of interests like meditation (of which mindfulness is one version), burning incense, spiritual healing, past lives, and other similar stuff. And if I'm being honest, and without putting too fine a point on it, just as f*cked up as everyone else.

Whatever the practices they indulged in that made them *spiritual* people, it hadn't healed them. Or at least it hadn't yet. Some were genuinely lovely people, but some were struggling while pretending everything was great. This isn't a criticism. Many of us do this – me included, at times. It's human.

In comparison, some of the nicest and most well-rounded people I have ever known were in the corporate job I had left a year earlier – and they'd never lit a candle, burned incense, chanted mantras, nor stepped foot in a church, unless it was raining and they needed shelter.

I began to wonder if people are drawn to spiritual practices like meditation because they need help, not because they are advanced beings and meditation is just something that advanced people do. I had previously assumed it was the latter, because that's the impression some of the spiritual people I knew gave.

But as I said, most people, I came to realize in time, are drawn to meditation and other spiritual practices because they need them, not because they are already free of all the baggage that life asks us to carry, or because they're elevated beings.

I had also assumed that being spiritual, where meditation is usually an integral part, made you a kinder person. Softer. Gentler. More compassionate. That seemed to be the case with the handful of

Buddhist teachers I knew whose training had included how to be kindful. But I realized it's not true in general.

Cue the email I received at around that time.

Basically, whatever you believe in, spiritually or religiously, is independent of what you do. The belief is in your head, whether you believe in God, five gods, or no god at all. What matters is your actions, and that's that. They're what make you and the people around you feel good or not. If 'spiritual' comes with some compassion and kindness, awesome. If it doesn't... run.

Now, people take up meditation for very different reasons. For some, it's to help them deal with stress. For others, it's to help their concentration. There are people who find it helps them sleep better, or to manage their emotions, even to help them deal with anxiety or depression. And there are those for whom it's about personal or spiritual growth.

Here are some of the main reasons and benefits. Research studies have been done on all these, but I won't beat you around the head with them and there isn't a test at the end. You'll have to take my word for it. There you go, being kind already!

1. Stress reduction

One of the most common reasons people take up mindfulness meditation is to reduce stress. If you ever feel like a pressure cooker about to blow, it can be your off-switch.

2. Living in the now

Meditation can be like giving your mind a GPS to the present moment. No more time-traveling to the past or future!

3. A remote control for your busy mind

Goldfish attention span? Occasionally feel like someone is playing with the remote and your mind is the TV? Meditation can help you take control of it and stick to one channel at a time. It helps you swap channel surfing for laser focus. In effect, it can help your attention level up to dolphin status.

4. Emotional well-being

Meditation can make you feel brighter inside and out. It can help you form an improved self-image, a more positive outlook on life, and master that skill of surfing emotional waves rather than being overwhelmed by them.

5. Increased self-awareness

Ever heard the term, 'know thyself'? Meditation can be like having a 'Get to Know Me' session without the expensive therapy. It can help you form a better understanding of yourself. With this enhanced insight, you're better able to control how you are with people and how you respond to some of life's challenges.

6. Reduced symptoms of anxiety and depression

Mindfulness meditation can help to keep the mind gremlins at bay and to manage symptoms related to anxiety, depression, and panic attacks. It helps us take control of a potentially spiraling mind by giving us the ability to take a step back and view stuff from a different perspective.

7. Addiction

Some people find that meditation is a really helpful way to control addictive behaviors. It can bring your mind to the moment to increase self-control and an awareness of triggers. It's like having a Houdini in your head when you feel chained by certain behaviors.

8. Better sleep

Some people count sheep, others meditate. This is because it enables them to relax and take control of a wandering mind. It then helps them fall asleep faster and enjoy deeper, more restorative sleep.

9. Physical health

For some, meditation is like a mind spa and a body spa all in one. It's been linked to improved physical health, like lowered blood pressure, reduced symptoms of irritable bowel syndrome, and a healthier immune system.

10. Spiritual growth

For people looking to connect to the cosmic Wi-Fi, some find that meditation gives them the password. It helps them to feel connected and deepen their understanding of life's mysteries.

11. Cognitive enhancement

Some practice meditation to build their brain power, or to better flex their mental muscles. Certain practices can enhance cognitive functions, such as memory and processing speed.

12. Managing pain

There are people who meditate for pain relief. Mindful breathing can help reduce the perception of pain in the brain and be used as part of a pain management regimen.

13. Enhanced creativity

Some find that meditation helps get their creative juices flowing. By quietening mental chatter and helping access a deeper state, they feel it helps them unlock their inner artist or writer.

14. Personal growth and self-discipline

Many take up meditation as a form of personal growth because it teaches patience, discipline, and commitment. And according to some, if you want to have the self-discipline of a ninja, then meditation is your guru.

I was only going to list a few reasons and benefits, but once I got going I thought you'd rather have the fuller picture anyway. All the same, there's nothing about kindness on that list and this book is about giving a f*ck, why it's pretty cool to be giving a f*ck, how giving a f*ck is the new black, who and what we could be giving our f*cks about, why it actually benefits our mental health, and also why we should be practicing the art of giving a f*ck about ourselves too.

What I could have added to the above list is this: For some people, mindfulness meditation can actually make them self-absorbed. But I said the list was about benefits and that isn't really a benefit – more like a drawback. I'll explain it all in the next chapter.

Now, I love mindfulness and I practice it myself, but this is where I want to make a pitch for *kindfulness*.

Partly it's because I like the word – I use it a lot, and I think it would be brilliant if it found its way into the dictionary (here's looking at you, dictionary editors!) – but there's more to it than a great-sounding word. For you dictionary editors out there, I've defined kindfulness good and proper in the next chapter to save you the trouble of having to think it up all by yourselves.

Anyway, despite the similarity in the word, kindfulness is not exactly a reinvention of mindfulness. Rather, it's an expansion of it. It marries the awareness of mindfulness, so you get all the good juice from mindfulness, with the tender embrace of kindness. It essentially supercharges the experience.

Where mindfulness says, 'Notice,' kindfulness whispers, 'And also care.' It nudges us not only to be present with our experiences, but to infuse them with a warm-hearted understanding.

But it's not just a practice like mindfulness meditation. That is one form of kindfulness. It's much more. It brings mindfulness back into bed with kindness, because it's also about being mindfully kind as we go about our lives.

Notice where you can offer a helping hand, who you can help. It doesn't need to be much. Buy someone a coffee. Let someone go in front of you in the queue for the checkout if you have a trolley-load of stuff and that kid only has a banana and a packet of chewing gum. Sometimes, just a smile or a polite nod is enough.

How mindfulness can make you selfish

As you'll now know, I'm quite into mindfulness. It's like a workout for my brain, and I raved about its perks at the end of the previous chapter. But if we're talking about making our world – this giant floating rock in space that we all share – a bit friendlier, then mindfulness alone might not cut it.

Traditional mindfulness was all about being a top-notch human, but once it ditched its old-school spiritual vibes, it lost some of that 'be nice to everyone' memo.

Now, I'm not trash-talking mindfulness. For some, it's a game-changer. It's like unplugging from the Matrix. Suddenly, you're stopping to smell the roses, lulled by birdsong and the buzzing of bees, even enchanted by the sweet harmonies in a crowded room. But while mindfulness may give you enhanced spidey senses, it doesn't exactly hand out kindness badges.

It makes you notice more. Whether you act on what you notice or not, that's down to you. And empathy has something to do with it.

Enter 'kindfulness.' Think of it as Mindfulness 2.0. If you dive into the world of kindness – why it rocks, its health perks, its anti-blue-mood powers – it's like leveling up. When you're kind-hearted and practice mindfulness, then it's like you've got this built-in GPS pointing you toward doing good.

But here's the twist: Without the kindness chip, mindfulness can sometimes backfire. Some folks might end up not-so-nice. Still, you don't have to take my word for it; the science is all there.

The three chairs experiment

Researchers hooked a bunch of people up with a meditation app and asked them to do mindfulness meditation over the following three weeks. Then they called them into the lab one at a time. They said it was for a cognitive test, but it was really a hidden-camera-style experiment. They'd set up a fake scenario.

Each person had to sit in a waiting area when they arrived. It had three chairs. Two were already taken, so their only option was to take the single remaining seat. As I said, it was a set-up. The seats were occupied by a couple of members of the research team.

A minute later, a girl turned up. She was also one of the research team but in disguise – on crutches and wearing a medical moon boot. She made painful winces from time to time so that everyone could see she was suffering. The people in the occupied seats barely acknowledged her. They'd been instructed to fake disinterest.

Would the people who'd learned mindfulness meditation offer to give up their seat for her? Indeed they did! Thirty-seven percent of those folks who did mindfulness offered her their seat, compared with only 14 percent of those who didn't meditate. Go mindfulness!

But, as I said earlier, it wasn't that mindfulness made them kinder. It's that it took them out of their own heads and made them take notice.

Here's the thing. Empathy is usually where kindness starts. We empathize with a person's plight and we feel moved to help them. That's when we have compassion: It's empathy with a motivation to help. Then we do something – we carry out an act of kindness. Empathy becomes compassion, which becomes kindness, like a seed growing into a flower.

The researchers had carried out a previous experiment where half the people did mindfulness and half did a compassion-based meditation – and both groups helped the girl equally, so the natural assumption was that mindfulness must be increasing empathy and compassion. However, it hadn't done so in this case, at least not in three weeks. When they measured people's levels of empathy afterward, there wasn't any difference between those who had meditated and the ones who hadn't.

As I said, mindfulness doesn't make us kinder; it helps us notice.

Mind stretching

Empathy is usually a starting point for kindness. It's your 'I-feel-with-you' meter. Some call it the stock in friendship soup. It's the first step before a hug; you've got to feel before you squeeze, so to speak. It's usually only once you empathize with someone's situation that you feel moved to help them.

In the above study, the researchers measured how much empathy participants had *after* they did the practice. This is a form of empathy called empathic accuracy. It shows how good you are at picking up on someone's needs.

If the researchers had measured how much empathy the people had to begin with, then that's a different thing altogether: It would be their levels of dispositional empathy, which is sometimes known as 'trait' empathy. It's what's in your personality.

Now, here's an important question that some researchers had: Would people naturally high in dispositional empathy be kinder after mindfulness than people low in empathy?

In an experiment carried out by a different group of researchers, participants had their dispositional empathy measured and then some were taught mindfulness meditation, some listened to classical music, and some attended two lectures on empathy and giving help to others. The latter two groups were included for comparison purposes.

Afterward, they were all presented with a situation. This time, it wasn't the crutches and moon boot scenario. Instead, they listened to a fake radio interview about a girl named Anna. Anna was having a crappy time. She'd just lost her job. And she had a disability. Besides all that going on, she was trying to complete her undergrad degree.

The question was how much the participants would care about Anna's situation. How willing would they be to help a real-life Anna after practicing mindfulness? And would this relate to their level of dispositional empathy?

The results were clear. Again, mindfulness was linked with kind behavior. More people were kind after practicing mindfulness than if they'd listened to Beethoven or watched a TED talk on empathy. But here's the caveat: That was only the case if you were high in empathy.

As I said earlier, the scientists had measured dispositional empathy to begin with. It turned out that mindfulness only increases kind behavior if you're already high in empathy.

And here's the stinker: If you're low in empathy, mindfulness meditation seems to have the opposite effect. It makes you less kind and more self-absorbed. Even though mindfulness helps us notice more, it's down to our empathy levels whether we'll act on what we notice or not.

After practicing mindfulness, people low in empathy gave even less of a f*ck and were less likely to help those like Anna than people who hadn't done any mindfulness at all.

So what it comes down to is this: Whether mindfulness results in kindness has less to do with mindfulness itself and more to do with our existing personality. Even though it sharpens our alertness and gives us enhanced spidey senses, our natural empathy is the deciding factor on whether we'll help others or not. Mindfulness acts like a stretching exercise, only for the mind instead of the body. It extends us further into who we already are.

Another way to look at it, as some researchers have argued, is that it stretches you in the direction of your personal values. If your values include empathy, kindness, friendship, honesty, dependableness – things like that – then yes, mindfulness will make you kinder.

But if they don't – if your values are more about personal achievement, competence, strength, that sort of stuff – then there's a good chance that mindfulness will make you more self-absorbed. And from that self-absorbed state, you're far less likely to notice the pregnant woman on the train who needs a seat, the person approaching the door as you let it close mindlessly, or the elderly guy at the store who's struggling to reach a box of cornflakes on the top shelf.

Mindfulness is a bit like a mind-selfie. It gives you a snapshot of who you are, but on the inside. Except that it also enlarges the image.

If you're a kind person, it will tease kindness out of you even more. Great! As I said, I love mindfulness and there are a lot of kind people out there who become kinder when they practice it.

But if you're not naturally kind, the opposite can happen. Or, as some scholars have noted, people who are self-absorbed become even more self-absorbed. Narcissists who practice mindfulness become more narcissistic.

This was cross-checked with some other research and the authors even wrote of the result: 'Mindfulness backfired among those who seemed to need it the most.' People who were narcissistic became less empathetic after a short mindfulness session – less kind and more self-absorbed.

There are, of course, some limitations in the above pieces of research and I don't want to gloss over this.

Offering up a seat to someone isn't the same as giving money or doing volunteer work, for example, so we can't take these results as if they absolutely 100 percent apply to every real-life situation. But there's enough research to show us that it's likely to be generally true. Also, while some people with autistic traits tend to be lower in empathy, the above cross-checking paper found that people with higher levels of autistic traits actually became kinder after mindfulness.

How you see the world

So there we have it. It's all about empathy. Case closed. Or is it? Could there be another layer? You'd think that now scientists have a result they'd be done with it. But that's not how things work in science. If there are a few unanswered questions, stuff that doesn't quite fit the mold, we usually like to poke our noses around a bit more to get to the bottom of it.

Because as with many things in life, there are often two or more sides to any situation. On the issue of whether mindfulness makes us kinder or less so, it turns out that some of it comes down to our perspective on the world.

Some of us look at life through rose-tinted spectacles – and I admit that I'm one of those people. Annoying, I know. Friends have pointed out as much. 'No rain, no flowers' – that's my mantra. It has to be when you live somewhere it rains a lot. But I think it's better than viewing the world with suspicion. It's been said that a pickpocket in a room full of saints only sees pockets and misses out on all the kindness floating about the place.

It turns out that how you see the world and your place in it plays a role in whether mindfulness makes you kinder or not. It's what psychologists term your 'self-construal.'

In 2021, Michael Poulin from the State University of New York at Buffalo did a study that tapped into this. He explored two self-construals (ways that people perceive themselves in relation to others): independent and interdependent. The main difference between them is that for people with an independent self-construal, it's mostly about *me*, whereas for people with an interdependent self-construal, it's more about *us*.

Generally speaking, Western cultures (like the USA, UK, and Western Europe) lean toward the independent side, whereas Asian cultures (like India and China, where Buddhist thought originated) lean toward the interdependent. I say 'generally speaking' because there's a mixture within any culture and most people have characteristics of both, just like we have mixed characteristics of extroversion and introversion. We usually lean more toward one or the other, so we refer to ourselves as *either* extroverted *or* introverted. But the truth is that we have a blend of both flavors. Similarly, we're all part-independent, part-interdependent, but we tend to lean more one way than the other. And whether we show more of one or the other depends on our context.

Even within cultures, different groups have different leanings. Racial minorities in the USA are more interdependent than Whites. And something similar is true between classes: The working classes are more interdependent than those in the middle classes. Again, this is generally speaking.

But let's get back to Poulin's experiment, which involved 366 college students, mindfulness, and... some envelopes. After their mindfulness session, participants were told about a charity for poor and homeless people. The university wished to send letters to alumni, asking if they could make a donation. Would the participants like to stay behind and help stuff some envelopes?

This was the kindness test. The aim was to see if self-construal influenced kind behavior. And guess what? It did.

Participants with an interdependent view stuffed 17 percent more envelopes after their mindfulness meditation (remember, interdependent is more about 'us'), while the independent ones (it's more about 'me') stuffed 15 percent fewer. In fact, those with the independent view stuffed fewer envelopes than the control group who hadn't done any mindfulness at all. As with the empathy studies, mindfulness meditation resulted in some people becoming less kind than they would have been had they not done any mindfulness at all.

Mindfulness seems to amplify our natural tendencies. Community-minded people become more helpful, while people who are more self-focused tend to become even more so. Again, mindfulness meditation stretches us further in the direction of who we are.

Here's the troubling thing. In the West, as we know, our dominant view is independent. It's ingrained into us from childhood: to distinguish ourselves, to rise up, to be the best. Individualism is emphasized. Could this mean that even though mindfulness is helping us chill, manage stress, and flex resilience, it's also making many of us less kind and that we'd be better off not doing it at all?

Well, not necessarily. There's dispositional empathy, as we learned earlier. You can lean toward the independent end of the scale and be high in empathy, or lean toward the interdependent and be low in empathy. It's a mixture of factors.

Also, there are mindfulness teachers who offer the full-course meal. They emphasize being mindful as you go about your life. The way they teach leans more toward traditional mindfulness than modern app versions. They encourage students not only to practice mindfulness meditation, but to be mindful of how they feel, what they say, and of their behavior, with a view to introducing more conscious awareness in life and more kindness and compassion as they interact with people.

We have to remember that Poulin was carrying out a controlled experiment, which used stuffing charity envelopes as a measure of kind behavior. That's not the same as offering a seat to a girl who is walking with crutches, or helping someone like a real-life Anna who's in immediate need of assistance, or generally thinking kindly of people, for that matter.

The gist of these studies is that they show that mindfulness meditation seems to tilt the scales toward our core selves... whatever our core selves may be. So, it's not just about empathy, nor is it only about our self-construal. It's a bit of both.

Now, if our self-construals aren't set in stone, and we can shift our viewpoint, this could have implications for kindness and society. The next part of the study tested this idea by using a technique called priming.

Priming

Priming is where you subtly plant an idea in a person's mind and then they think they've come up with it themselves. A lot of stage performers do it.

I once experimented with priming at a family birthday a few years ago in quite a spectacular way. It was my dad's 70th and his siblings had come to our house to enjoy the celebrations with us. I sat with one of Dad's sisters for a bit and chatted.

Now, while I'd like to say I was being sociable, I had an ulterior motive. I intentionally planted the idea of a card in her mind – the queen of hearts. Several times during our conversation, I happened to mention the *queen*, as in the late Queen Elizabeth II, and I found a way to say the word *heart* a handful of times by referring to my former work in cardiovascular research and development (R&D).

A short while later, I took a deck of cards out of the drawer and announced to everyone that I was going to do a card trick for a wee bit of entertainment. That, or I would sing a song. (I'd had a few glasses of wine.) They went for the card trick. Phew!

I put my hands up, circled around for effect, and announced to everyone, 'OK, pick a card, any card, first one that pops into your head, just shout it out.' Only, I looked at Dad's sister when I said to shout it out.

She blurted, 'Queen of hearts!' Of course she did. Priming!

I then flexed the deck a few times for effect and threw the whole thing at the window. It made a huge noise and cards flew all over the place. Everyone got a fright. But when they looked... there was the queen of hearts stuck right on the glass.

It freaked everyone out, if I'm being honest. My sister Lesley went over to get it off the window and was freaked out even more. She trilled, 'It's on the other side! It went right through the window and it's on the other side!'

Naturally, about half an hour earlier, I'd snuck outside and stuck the queen of hearts to the window with a piece of sticky tape. As I said, stage performers do this sort of thing all the time. They're a bit cooler than me and they do it in really fancy and elaborate ways, but the idea is more or less the same. Priming.

Anyhow, back to the Poulin study. They primed a set of volunteers with either a more independent or interdependent view. So, regardless of their initial orientation, they were going to be thinking more in terms of whichever self-construal Poulin had primed them with.

The result? Mindfulness made people kinder when they'd been primed with an interdependent view and made them less kind when they were primed with an independent view. In other words, self-construal is pliable. Even for things that seem set in our personality, we can change them.

But this isn't really about labels, and it transcends empathy or self-construal. In a world that seems to be spinning faster and faster, and where time and time again a mountain of shit seems to hit the fan, it's about learning to recognize that it's not all about *me*. It's about *us*.

No person is an island. And no country is an island. OK, geographically that might be the case, but you know what I mean. We're all on this Earth together. We're family, whether we like it or not. Even though this is typically an interdependent view, it's about more than the label. It's about recognizing that there's more to life than our own successes and achievements.

It would be nice if we cared about more than our own health and happiness and it'd be nice if we cared about other people's too. In certain African cultures there's a philosophical concept called 'Ubuntu.' The word comes from the Nguni Bantu languages and the Zulu proverb 'Umuntu ngumuntu ngabantu.' It translates to 'a person is a person through other person.' Or 'I am because you are.' It embodies the idea that our humanity is deeply tied to our relationships with others. It says that our actions and attitudes should be guided by compassion, empathy, and mutual respect.

By kindness.

Can we learn empathy?

It turns out that just as we can shift our self-construals, we can learn empathy. And it doesn't need priming. The whole 'walk a mile in someone else's shoes' pretty much captures it. Let me offer a real-world example.

Dozens of asylum seekers died when their boat crashed on Christmas Island in 2010. Yet the first thought of Raye Colbey was: 'Serves you bastards right. Come the right way and it wouldn't have happened.' Hers was typical of a general sentiment toward asylum seekers.

When a detention center was built in her neighborhood in the Adelaide Hills, she was categorically against it. She had spent 20 years working with intellectually disabled children. How dare these asylum seekers get funding and resources that disadvantaged Australians needed more. She hated them with such intensity, she said, that it was eating her like a disease.

She voiced her opinions at a town meeting and was subsequently invited to be part of a documentary called *Go Back to Where You Came From*, produced by SBS in Australia. It would take her and others on a 25-day journey that would trace in reverse the journey many refugees make to reach Australia from Africa and Malaysia.

She first found herself in Wodonga, where she was greeted by seven kind and smiling faces: Bahati and Maisara Masudi and their five sons aged between 16 years and just seven months. It turned out they'd waited nine years in a refugee camp before being settled in Wodonga only 18 months earlier. Raye was to live with them for the next six days, these people that she had admitted she hated.

She changed during those days.

Learning about the atrocities the family had faced, the struggles they had endured, the terrible things that they had gone through, she found an empathy she didn't have for them before. She heard of the rape, torture, and murder that had become commonplace in the country they once called home.

In an interview with the *Sydney Morning Herald* afterward, she explained her emotions were now in turmoil. She said she was 'overwhelmed by the degree of intense cruelty and persecution that you only read about or see on TV.'

'Here I was,' she said, 'immersed in the lives of true refugees. And I was struggling.

'At night, as I lay on the hard floor, unable to sleep, the reality of following in the footsteps of a refugee was sinking in. I wept for their pain and suffering.

'Was it a crime to want a life of peace, to raise children and watch them grow and develop?'

The experience fundamentally changed her. She had much more empathy and compassion afterward. So much so that whenever she heard about protests at detention centers, she got angry. 'These people are desperate,' she'd shout – a complete turnaround from how she'd felt just a few months earlier.

Sometimes, all it takes is more information for our empathy dial to shift. That's why we're asked to first walk a mile in someone else's shoes, as the saying goes. When we more deeply consider a person's actual plight, empathy begins to kindle in us. It's part of what it is to be human.

We're all members of one family. Human*kind*. Our world would be better if we really started acting like it.

Mindfulness plus kindness

As I said, back in the day, one of the goals of traditional mindfulness was to help people become better people, and to give a f*ck about other people as well as themselves. The Buddha said as much, only he used the language of the times. After all, the actual f*ck word hadn't been invented then. It only appeared a few thousand years later, possibly when an apple landed on Sir Isaac Newton's head, but it's hard to know for sure.

Despite its other successes, mindfulness light doesn't achieve all that traditional mindfulness set out to do. But what if kindness and compassion were taught as *part of* mindfulness meditation, just like they were when Buddha was sitting under the Bodhi tree? It might just make us kinder. By bringing the kindness back into mindfulness, mindfulness becomes kindfulness.

So, researchers did something along these lines. They compared the usual practice of mindfulness against mindfulness that also included a couple of lessons on kindness and ethics. The researchers called it SecularM versus EthicalM. M is for mindfulness, in case you were wondering. We scientists can be a creative bunch!

The researchers recruited 621 volunteers for the study and all the participants practiced daily mindfulness for six days. The difference, however, was that the

EthicalM participants were also guided toward having loving and kind thoughts, taught about not harming people or animals, and about how we're all connected and our actions therefore have consequences – sort of a condensed summary of the Eightfold Path. And some of their mindfulness exercises focused on compassion and kindness.

As before, the final test was to see who would respond to a situation asking for kindness. They were told a fake story about someone in need, along the lines of the Anna story spun to the previous group of meditators, and then given the opportunity to make a donation to charity.

The outcome: Team EthicalM gave more than Team SecularM. Those extra lessons about kindness made all the difference. And as with other studies, it was also dependent on dispositional empathy. Across the board in both teams, people high in empathy gave more than people low in empathy. The silver lining was that those who got the kindness lessons gave more than those who didn't, and this was even true of people low in empathy. When mindfulness was infused with kindness, everyone became a little kinder.

What does this mean? It means that kindness shifts all of us at the base. Regardless of empathy, core values, or self-construal, learning a bit about kindness and why it matters makes all of us a wee bit nicer to each other. It guides the sharper ninja focus and awareness that are cultivated by mindfulness. It focuses our inner

GPS so that when we do mindfulness, or anything for that matter, it points us a bit more in the kind direction. Learning even just a little about kindness in any pursuit brings a little more heart and make us more mindfully kind.

What is kindfulness?

OK, before we move on to the next chapter, I just want to make it clear that I'm not saying we need to ditch mindfulness meditation. Far from it. Mindfulness is good for us and healthy for all those different reasons I gave at the end of the Chapter 1. Also, mindfulness itself is about more than mindfulness meditation. It encompasses being mindful as you go about your day. Some mindfulness teachers place as much focus, in fact, on this as they do on the seated meditation practice, just as Jon Kabat-Zinn did originally.

Mindfulness meditation *can* make us more alert to opportunities for kindness, because it makes us more mindfully aware. But whether we act on these opportunities is down to us.

Enter kindfulness, which is:

1. Being mindfully kind as we go through our lives. It's about being kind on purpose, because kindness is the right thing to do in a particular moment. And this also includes self-kindfulness – being kind to yourself. (I'll talk more about this later.)

2. Any mindfulness-based practice where part of the focus is kindness or compassion, rather than just on the breath, body, or mind (which is mindfulness). It can be both: focusing on the breath but also giving a little time for some kind and compassionate thoughts. (I've popped a few kindfulness practices in Appendix II.)

3. Learning mindfulness while also having a little education about kindness: What it is, why it matters, the difference it can make, how it impacts health. It prompts us to bring kindness to mind from time to time before we do any meditation practice, to help orient our inner compass.

There we have it. Mindfulness is great, but with a wee sprinkle of kindness it becomes even greater. Learning about kindness and even bringing it to mind before we practice mindfulness can help orient our moral compass. It sets our inner GPS to empathy and kindness. That way, we increase our tendency to be kind in life.

In fact, kindness has a lot more up its sleeve. It can do wonders for your mental health, as we'll learn in the next chapter.

A superfood for your mental health

Everyone today has heard of superfoods – those magical ingredients we sprinkle onto our smoothies or toss into salads; the blueberries, kale, and chia seeds that promise to boost our physical well-being. We diligently chase after these nutrient powerhouses because we know they're good for our bodies. But there's a 'superfood' for your mental health as well. Only, it doesn't come from the aisles of a health food store or the depths of the Amazon rainforest.

Cue kindness.

Imagine for a moment that you're having a crappy day. Everything seems to be going wrong, and there's an annoying gray cloud hovering over your head that just won't budge. But then someone – maybe a colleague, a friend, even a stranger on the street – shows you a simple act of kindness.

Perhaps they lend you a listening ear, hand you some flowers or a thank-you note for something you said last week, or even offer you a seat on a crowded bus. Instantly, there's a ray of sunshine piercing through that cloud. Your day isn't as gloomy as it was just a moment ago.

It's also a little brighter for the colleague, friend, or stranger who offered you that ray of sunshine. Kindness benefits the giver as well as the receiver. It even benefits anyone who witnesses it. Kindness is a win–win–win. The truth is, acts of kindness – whether given, received, or witnessed – aren't just fleeting moments of happiness. They're potent elixirs that have profound and lasting impacts on our mental health.

Kindness isn't only sweet, it's powerful. And the best part? It's readily available to all of us, anytime, anywhere. No blender required.

The power of service

A few years back, I lost a dear friend, Margaret. She was something else, always with a heart full of kindness, thoughtful gestures, and an infectious laugh. We'd chat for hours, and every so often she'd share tales of her battle with severe depression.

One of the moments she'd recall happened after a particularly tough bout resulted in her attempting suicide. She then spent some time in a psychiatric ward. Shortly after her release from hospital, she'd sent a fax to Patch Adams, the doctor who believes in the healing power of laughter. She had just watched a heart-warming movie about his life, with Robin Williams bringing Patch's character to life.

Margaret would always beam when she recounted how, on the very same day she sent the fax, Patch responded. She would emphasize, 'On the same day!' It was clear to her that he genuinely cared.

In that heartfelt note, Patch shared a piece of his own journey, revealing his own brush with suicidal thoughts. His advice was simple yet transformative: 'Go out and serve and see your depression lift.'

Inspired, Margaret and her husband, Kenny, plunged into volunteer work with a local befriending charity. They decided to be that ray of sunshine for others struggling with their mental health. And let me tell you, their efforts created ripples. Some of the people they helped through the befriending charity turned into lifelong friends.

What Patch said truly worked wonders for Margaret. Helping others became her beacon, illuminating her path with joy and purpose. I met her not long after this transformation, and she was honestly one of the most cheerful souls I've ever known. She even teamed up with Patch, training as a laughter therapist, and embarked on some amazing journeys, dressed up as a clown, spreading giggles in care homes and children's hospitals. The effect the pair of them had was like magic. It's stories like hers that made me really understand the profound connection between kindness and mental well-being.

Kindness: It's in our DNA

Kindness feels good, whether you're the one doing the good deed, getting the helping hand, or just watching it all go down. But why are we like this – drawn to being nice? The answer lies way back, millions of years ago.

Our ancient relatives figured out that sharing was the thing to do; there were no stores around, so they lived in interdependent communities. They learned there's safety in numbers. They teamed up, helped each other out, and looked after their little ones together. And it meant the human race thrived.

This inclination got passed from one generation to the next, and the next, and the next. That feeling you get of 'Yep, this is the right thing to do'? That's Mother Nature giving us a high five. It's her way of saying, 'Good job for keeping the human race going!'

Here's another fun fact: We have kindness genes. They're ancient, like 100-million-years-old kind of ancient, and we can trace their roots back around 700 million years. Evolutionary scientists now tell us that, as the tendency for kindness grew stronger in our species over time, four distinct reasons began to emerge:

1. Family love (kin altruism)

We're basically wired to be good to our closest relatives. Think about it: Parents are always fussing over their kids, and siblings often have each other's backs (even after the occasional squabble). I recently helped my sister to move house: That's family love doing its magic! It's like our built-in radar for spreading love, empathy, and that warm fuzzy feeling in the family. It makes all of us stronger.

2. Community vibes (mutualism)

Way back when, sticking together meant not getting eaten by wild animals. There's safety in numbers. Fast forward to today, and we've still got this 'together is better' mentality. It's why we create clubs, cheer for the same sports teams, or belt out the national anthem. It's all about loyalty, bonding, and a 'we're in this together' spirit. Each time you feel camaraderie at a group outing, ancient community vibes are at play!

3. You scratch my back... (reciprocal altruism)

This is like an invisible tally we keep. It's not intentional, more instinctual: I help you out today, and maybe you'll help me tomorrow. Not that we're always calculating – it's more like an automatic trust thing. Like if your car broke down and your neighbor offered you a lift to work. A few weeks later, she's going on holiday and you offer to keep an eye on her house. Your neighbor helped you out of pure kindness, but at the back of her mind she's aware that you'll probably help her out sometime. It's about trust, friendship, and that satisfying sense of 'I got you.'

4. Kindness show-off (competitive altruism)

OK, sometimes we do good things because, let's be honest, we want to shine a bit. We want to be the star player in a team sport. But it's not always about bragging rights – sometimes it's about that inner drive to be genuinely generous or heroic. But, hey, if you do get a little boost in your social standing or a few extra brownie points, that's just a bonus. Deep down, we might hope it makes us look good, even if we're not consciously thinking that way, but it's also about that deep-seated urge to do good.

Now, I know that some of this makes it sound like we're just being kind for the rewards. But let's be real. Most of us aren't thinking, 'What's in it for me?' when we do a kind act. It's just... natural. Instinctual. It's simply part of our deep innate psychology that evolved in the human psyche to aid the survival of our species. The fact it comes with a good feeling is Mother Nature giving us a high five for it.

So let's not get too caught up in the reasons why we're kind. The academics can squabble about that. Just get on with doing your own thing with a bit of heart. The bottom line is that kindness is innate to us. It's deep in our DNA. Kind is what we are.

Be kind for happy, colorful vibes

In his 1979 book *The Healing Power of Doing Good*, Allan Luks, Director at the Center for Nonprofit Leaders at Fordham University, coined the term 'helper's high.' He was studying the habits and experiences of over 3,000 people who did volunteer work. When he looked at his data, he discovered that over 95 percent of people get some form of a high when they help someone: Helper's high is that warm, fuzzy, satisfying feeling.

He also found that people who help others regularly are much more likely to be in good health than those who don't. Yep, this is Nature's reward again. She keeps us healthy because kindness is important for the survival of all of us.

Loads of research since Luks's work has backed up his observations. It's not only concluded that kindness make us happier but that it helps fortify our minds against depression and anxiety. Kindness is like a mental health pill.

Nowadays, scientists will typically ask a bunch of people to do a rough number of acts of kindness over the course of a day, week, month, or some other period of time. Then they'll measure how happy they are. Their happiness is then compared with how they were before they did the kind things or against other people who just behaved normally during that time. Does kindness make them happier?

Every version of the research says it does – even if you feel pretty crappy to begin with. Kindness lifts us out of ourselves. In the moment that you help someone, your attention shifts away from your own troubles and onto the immediate needs of someone else. It taps into that ancient knowing; it's a stir in our DNA. It's like effervescent bubbles of rightness float to the surface and give a little tickle to your heart.

And it helps you see the world differently, more brightly. Nearly everyone has had the experience that sadness washes some of the color out of life. Everything around us seems to take on a gray monotone wash. That's not just a feeling. It's a real thing. Negative emotions impact the processing of color in the brain. They can cause colors to appear less vibrant. On the other hand, positive emotions, like the lift we get from kindness, help us see colors more richly. In other words, when you're kind, you not only feel lighter, you also see the world brighter.

Money can buy happiness... when you give it away

Scientists at the University of British Columbia in Canada once asked 632 people to make a daily record of how they spent their money over a month. They asked them to list everything – from paying bills, to shopping, eating lunch, giving donations to charity, buying gifts for others, treating themselves to a pair of jeans or a spa day, paying for coffee with a friend or fuel for the car, buying a packet of chewing gum, a bunch of bananas, and a bottle of water. Everything.

The happiest people, it turned out, were the ones whose lists included spending some money on others. The scientists wondered if it mattered how much you spend on others. Let's face it, some people have a lot of spare cash while some have barely any at all. Surely Mother Nature won't reward wealthier people more than poor people.

So, they set up another study. This time, they gave volunteers either $5 or $20 and asked half of them to spend the money on others by the end of the day and the other half to spend it on themselves.

The result? At the end of that day, regardless of how much money they had been given at the start, if they had spent it on others, they were happier than if they had spent it on themselves. It didn't matter if you had $5 or $20. It wouldn't matter if it was $1 or $1 million.

And it helps sometimes if you know that what you're giving is having a positive effect. Researchers have found that giving money to charitable causes boosts happiness more when we understand how the money is going to be used by them.

Because the fact is that the actual money has nothing to do with it. It's the kindness that matters. Regardless of what is given, whether it's money, food, a treat, our time, support, or even our friendship, it's the giving itself that makes us happy, and there's a satisfaction we feel when we see, or even suspect there will be, a smile on the recipient's face.

A protective effect

Kindness can protect us against depression. According to research, there are much lower rates of depression among people who regularly volunteer than in the general population. Of course, it's fair to assume that some people volunteer because they are in good health, have spare time, and resources that enable them to volunteer. But even after accounting for this, it is also true that volunteering itself is a tonic.

Again, this is Nature's reward. Helping each other fortifies us. It builds a neurological and psychological sense of resilience in the face of everyday stressors, some of which might ordinarily have had unhealthy consequences.

In 2020, the Mental Health Foundation carried out a survey along these lines. They found that 63 percent of UK adults agreed that people being kind to others has a positive effect on their mental health.

Knowledge of the protective effect of kindness isn't new. It didn't even begin with Allan Luks, although he was one of the first to bring it to public attention in our modern era. In 1796, the English Quaker William Tuke declared that 'moral treatment' was a way of helping people with mental health problems. He had set up the York Retreat in the north of England, where patients came to live. At that time, people with mental health difficulties were usually locked away or suffered the seemingly inhumane and brutal asylums of the time. His own sister had experienced it.

But at the York Retreat, residents didn't receive any conventional treatments. Instead, they were encouraged to help each other; they were asked to look after the 'family' of other patients. The 'treatment' was kindness, expressed in trust, respect, and autonomy. They cooked and cleaned for each other. They lent listening ears. They played games. They mowed the lawn and watered flowers. They did everything for each other. And it worked. They all got better.

The York Retreat was so successful that the model of moral treatment was picked up in the USA. There, it gained huge popularity and spread through the country over the coming decades. Psychiatrists were so impressed by the gains their patients were making that they sincerely believed that moral treatment must somehow cause 'organic changes in brain matter.' Today, we know this to be true. A regular experience of kindness does alter brain circuits in positive ways that help to boost mood and counteract stress and anxiety.

Moral treatment had mostly been forgotten for a century or more... until now, for there is a growing interest in the scientific community. And the first results are in. The evidence is clear: There is now no question that kindness – whether given, received, or even witnessed – assists our mental health.

Organic changes in brain matter

Thanks to modern tech, we're now able to see how acts of kindness light up our brains. And it's a feel-good party up there. First off, when you have an experience of kindness your brain releases awesome chemicals such as dopamine, serotonin, oxytocin, and natural opiates such as endorphin. They're the brain's very own 'happy smoothie'!

Oxytocin, for example, is pretty amazing. It's a chain of nine amino acids, and I like to nickname it the 'kindness hormone' because it makes an appearance when you experience kindness. It's like when you're stressed out and your body releases stress hormones – only way more fun!

Funnily enough, it's not the actual acts of kindness or stressful events that trigger these hormones. It's how we *feel* about them and what the experiences are like for us. Imagine two friends stuck in traffic on their way to a big event. One's panicking, thinking they're doomed, and releasing a flood of stress hormones. The other is super chill, just vibing to the radio. Despite being in the same situation, only the stressed-out person is getting that stress hormone spike. The situation itself has little to do with the stress hormone spike, because the calm person isn't getting it. It's the *experience of stress* that produces stress hormones.

Similarly, if two people do a kind deed, but only one is really genuine about it, so feels all warm and fuzzy inside, guess who's getting a dose of the 'kindness hormone'? Yep, it's the warm and fuzzy one!

This is also why you don't necessarily need to be the giver of kindness to make kindness hormones. You can experience the upbeat feelings of kindness as the person who is receiving the good deed or even as someone watching it happen... even on a social media video.

In a sense, kindness hormones and stress hormones are *molecules of emotion*, to use a term coined by Candace Pert in her book of that name. Candace was a neuroscientist and pharmacologist who discovered how opiates such as endorphin bind in the brain. She noted that emotional experiences produce neuropeptides, and these then trigger physical changes in the body. In this way, emotional experiences often bring about physical effects throughout the body. Her research helped kick-start a whole new field where emotions, the brain, and the immune system all come together – psychoneuroimmunology. (A mouthful, I know! Most people call it PNI instead as it's easier to say.)

When you're kind, your brain releases feel-good chemicals such as dopamine, serotonin, oxytocin, and endorphin, and they give you that warm, satisfying feeling. It's like Nature's reward for being awesome.

Remember mindfulness? Regular mindfulness practice causes physical changes in the brain. It's like going to the gym and working out a muscle. Three things happen when you work out regularly. Muscles become firmer, larger, and more powerful. Something similar happens in the brain, although muscle growth doesn't quite fit when we're talking about this part of the body. Neuroplasticity is what scientists call it, but it's a similar sort of thing. When you practice mindfulness regularly, your brain regions become firmer (with more connections – like a tree growing more roots), larger, and more powerful. Instead of building biceps, you strengthen different parts of your brain.

Mindfulness practices pump up the brain's focus area (part of the forehead region, known as the dorsolateral prefrontal cortex), while kindness and compassion practices (kindfulness) build up happiness and empathy regions. The more you practice kindfulness, the more you experience these organic changes in brain matter and the happier and more empathetic you feel.

The warming spice in community soup

Ever dropped your wallet and someone picked it up for you, or been treated to lunch, or received an unexpected tip for a job well done? Or maybe someone brought you a cup of tea in bed. If so, you'll agree: There's a certain warmth to these gestures, and I'm not just talking about the tea.

Kindness is like that magical ingredient in life's soup. It has an amazing ability to make places and groups feel like home. Even if you're a newbie, an act of kindness can make you feel as if you've been part of the gang for years.

It's universal. Kindness transcends language barriers, cultural differences, and even those awkward social cues we sometimes miss. It's the one-size-fits-all jumper of human connection.

And it breeds trust. When someone extends a hand of kindness, it's as if they're saying, 'Hey, I've got your back.' It's a reassuring feeling, isn't it? Over time, these little gestures build up and lay down the bricks of trust.

Let's not forget that kindness creates ripples. Like a pebble dropped in a pond, these ripples spread out, touching shores far and wide. Similarly, one kind act can inspire another, creating a chain of goodwill and good vibes. Before you know it, everyone feels enveloped in a circle of warmth and belonging.

I say this because in a world that sometimes feels a bit too vast and disconnected, it's the little drops of kindness that draw us closer. These small, heartfelt, and honest gestures knit us closer together in the cozy quilt of community. Kindness isn't just about being nice – it's about making spaces where everyone feels they belong.

Doing kindness face to face can be especially beneficial. It adds that extra sprig of social connection.

For example, while donating to a charity can give you a boost (as well as helping those whom the charity supports), volunteering face to face can often do more for our mental health. In the same way, taking a friend for a coffee or cooking them dinner is better than sending them a coffee card or buying a meal voucher. Helping in ways that build social connection is like the spice in community soup.

An unexpected antidote to anxiety

Now here's something you probably don't know about me. I like coffee so much that I can't help using it in some of my analogies. OK, there are two things. The other is that I sometimes struggle with anxiety. I've felt this way on and off since I was a child. Imagine my satisfaction when I learned from experience that kindness can sometimes be an antidote to anxiety, whether you're the giver, receiver, or the observer.

Let's get back to those coffee analogies.... Say you're in a bustling coffee shop, the barista is frantically trying to keep up with the orders, people are tapping away on their laptops (usually me – I write my books in coffee shops), and there's that one person (there's always one!) talking way too loudly on their phone. There's an ambiance, though. That's one of the reasons I love writing in coffee shops.

All the same, I've known times when my anxiety comes on out of nowhere while I'm standing in the queue. But occasionally something remarkable happens. Someone has left money with the barista to pay for the next few people's coffees. That little act of kindness changes everything. Suddenly, the world doesn't seem as rushed, you get that warm glow inside, and you feel a strange sort of connection with the person who left the money with the barista. I've found it works the other way too. I've also left money with the barista, and it's given me a feel-good rush and a warm glow for ages.

But this isn't just about getting free coffee or making it free for someone else. Coffee has nothing to do with it, except that I wrote about this analogy while sipping a lovely cup of the black nectar. It's about kindness. Kindness can be that antidote to anxiety.

On a practical level, the way it works is that kindness lifts you out of yourself, whether you're the giver or receiver. If you've struggled with anxiety, you know what it's like. You're knee-deep in it and your thoughts can spiral and it feels like you're trapped in a whirlwind of 'what ifs.' No amount of rational thinking seems to help. Yet a bit of kindness can act as a gentle nudge that breaks that cycle.

It might be as simple as complimenting someone or helping a neighbor – or, as I said, leaving money with a barista to pay for the coffees of the next few customers. That act redirects your focus and before you know it, your anxiety has taken a backseat.

While this is happening, acts of kindness can trigger a release of oxytocin. This nifty little kindness hormone, also often also called the 'love hormone,' is brilliant at reducing anxiety and increasing feelings of trust and contentment. It actually dials down regions of the brain that are central to the experience of anxiety, like turning down a dimmer switch when the room is too bright. In essence, being kind is a bit like serving up a soothing mocktail for the soul.

Then there's connection. Anxiety can make us feel isolated, even if we're surrounded by a crowd. Yet kindness bridges that gap. It's one of the side effects of face-to-face kindness. It reminds us that we're all in this together and creates a sense of belonging. And when we feel connected, our anxiety often diminishes. Anxiety and feeling connected can't coexist; as you feel connected, your anxiety diminishes.

This was tested in a study of 115 highly anxious people. They were asked to do six acts of kindness a week for a month. At the end of that time, they felt better, were more satisfied in their relationships, and were less likely to avoid social interactions.

You see, when we're anxious, we imagine the worst-case scenarios in our interactions with people. But when we do face-to-face kind things, our interactions become more dominated by gratitude and positive moods. Through experience, this changes our expectation of what occurs in interactions.

So, I think we can all agree that even though life can at times be an overwhelming brew of complexities and anxieties, when we stir in some kindness, our cup usually tastes a bit sweeter.

OK, enough of the coffee analogies. That's what happens when I write in coffee shops.

A beautiful day in the neighborhood

I recently watched *A Beautiful Day in the Neighborhood*, where Tom Hanks plays Mr. Rogers. I have to admit that until I'd watched the movie, I didn't know all that much about Mr. Rogers. He's a household name in the USA, but not so much in the UK, where I live. But the movie really moved me. I'm a fan now!

Mr. Rogers, aka Fred Rogers, was a real-life kind-hearted man. He spent his days making children's TV, teaching everyone about being nice to each other and dealing with their feelings. Here's the interesting part – being so nice on TV wasn't just an act for him. He was a genuinely good person and loved helping people. He used to say that helping kids was the best bit of his life; it was a source of joy and good mental vibes for him. Plus, he'd visit kids in hospitals and even reply to fan mail personally. All these little acts of kindness not only warmed the hearts of others, they warmed his heart too. In a way, he showed us that being kind isn't just good for other people, it's good for your own soul.

Now let's talk about Lady Gaga. I'm a big fan, but not just of her music. She read one of my books on kindness and asked her charity, Born This Way Foundation, which she founded with her mum Cynthia, to reach out to me to see if there was any way we could work together.

Some time later, I spent a day with Cynthia and visited a project they helped with at a school on Long Island. The kids had been invited to use some of their Christmas allowance to buy presents for the children of women who were housed at a local women's shelter. When we arrived, the whole corridor was full of presents that the kids had bought. They then made a line and passed them all out to be loaded on a school bus. They had to squeeze in the presents at the end, such was the kids' generosity.

Afterward, the school asked the children to write about their experiences. How did helping others make them feel? What impact might the presents have on the homeless children? How can kindness change the world? That sort of thing.

Lady Gaga and Cynthia are champions for kindness and mental health. Gaga has been publicly open about her own struggles with anxiety and depression, but she decided to turn her experiences into something positive. That's why she created the Born This Way Foundation with her mom. They're all about spreading love and acceptance, especially for people facing mental health issues. Her foundation works hard to create safe spaces for young people, helping them feel accepted and supported.

While she's out there changing the world, Lady Gaga is also changing herself. She said that being kind and caring for others brings her happiness. It's like a double win: She helps people and it makes her feel a wee bit warmer inside too.

I'm not really one for name dropping, and I wasn't going to mention Lady Gaga or Cynthia at all, but I just deeply admire the work they do and their commitment to kindness and mental health in young people.

Children get a kick out of kindness

Kids are naturally sweet. They feel good helping out, just like most adults do. Some researchers at the University of British Columbia did a cool study with toddlers. They gave toddlers under two years old a puppet to play with. Sometimes, the toddlers got a treat, other times they were given treats to give to the puppet, and occasionally they were even asked to give the puppet a couple of their own treats.

The researchers wanted to know if giving made the children happier, like it does with adults. One of the ways we measure happiness in adults is by getting them to fill in fancy questionnaires. But with toddlers? Not so much. Instead, scientists watched their facial expressions as a general indicator of happiness.

They found the toddlers were happier when they shared their treats with the puppet than when they munched on the treats themselves. They were happiest of all when they gave their *own* treats to the puppet. Just like adults feel happier when they help others.

It works with older kids, too. Researchers asked some kids aged between nine and 11 to do some kind deeds for a few weeks. At the end, these kids were happier compared to kids who didn't join in on the kindness spree.

I've given talks in a few schools during what they call 'kindness week,' where each class focuses many of their activities on learning about, and doing, kindness. What they've seen is that when schools make a big deal about kindness, it can be a game-changer and even reduce bullying. Everyone feels better – both the kids being kind and the kids on the receiving end of kindness.

A handful of kindness studies with kids were conducted back in the 1970s and are almost forgotten about now, except among kindness researchers. In one, kids watched an episode from the TV show *Lassie* where Jeff, the main character, goes all out to save Lassie's puppies. Another group of children watched the episode but with this part cut out, for comparison purposes. After that, while playing a game to win points and prizes, they heard sounds of puppies in distress. Most of the kids who watched Jeff's heroism were like, 'We need to help those puppies!' and wanted to stop the game to go help, even though it meant losing their points and prizes.

If kindness is in our DNA, it's in children's DNA too

Kindness is in our DNA, and yep, that means kids, babies and toddlers have the gene too. Right from birth, kids have a basic sense of right and wrong. Think of it as their 'morality starter pack.' Researchers call it a 'first draft' of moral cognition. It's like kids inherit these kindness blueprints from our ancestors, who figured out that working together was way cooler than going solo. These first-draft principles are then shaped by the environment we grow up in.

Here's what's in their starter pack:

1. Fairness: Even infants expect people to play fair.

2. Avoidance of harm: Don't hurt others, simple as that.

3. In-group support (or 'family first'): They'll probably share their toys or sweets with their little brother or sister before they give it to a random kid.

4. Sense of authority: They understand there are certain people (like parents) who set the rules and they expect them to respond to and deal with transgressions.

Funnily enough, kids also know when to tweak these rules. They have an inbuilt sense of their hierarchy. Like, they're all for sharing (principle 1), but when things are scarce, they expect preferential treatment from their own group to override fairness (principle 3).

Some evolutionary biologists think this is because we've come to expect reciprocity from the people closest to us. They analyze this in energy terms, a bit like economists use monetary terms. If we're super kind to everyone all the time, then this might be too energy-costly. We'd wear ourselves out because we wouldn't get back enough energy to offset this energy cost. But if we are kinder to the people closest to us, we're more likely to get something back and our energy books are more likely to balance.

Of course, it's not like we all sit down with a calculator and plan this out – it's just a gut thing. It manifests in a sense of who to help first under certain types of conditions, and that's usually those closest to us.

As kids grow up, their idea of kindness gets a bit more detailed. Psychologists at King's College London and the University of Bath did research with five- and six-year-olds and found some interesting themes emerged in their ideas of kindness, what it means to them, and what motivates them to be kind. These were:

1. Doing things for others: Sharing toys, helping others.

2. Relating to others: Being friendly, playing, not leaving anyone out, and you know, not pushing people.

3. Rules and values: Being kind is awesome and the right thing, but maybe I don't need to be kind to 'bad' people.

4. Kindness affects us: Being nice makes you and others feel great, earns you friends, and it's contagious.

One last thing; kids can be really straightforward. In their interviews for the study, they said things like: 'My brother helps me with math and when I'm reading.' 'If someone is hurt you could give them a cuddle if they want one.' 'Be kind to everyone... even people in Japan and Spain and Portugal... and even Mrs. Jones, the Head Teacher.' 'Be kind to everyone, except for robbers... cos they might steal your stuff.'

Smile and the world smiles back at you

I used to know a guy who smiled at everyone. Well, not everyone, he told me. But nearly everyone. Sometimes you just know you shouldn't, he said.

Some people probably thought he was weird, but it was magical hanging out with him. Most people genuinely smiled back. Some were caught off guard as his smile and polite nod of the head lifted them out of whichever head space they were stuck in.

It was like a wee bit of sunshine followed him around. He told me that when people smile back, it gives him a lift for two reasons. One is the simple fact that a person is smiling in your direction. We innately feel good about this. It's like the universe is saying, 'Hello, you're doing great, you've got this.'

But the other is a sense that he's doing something good in the world, by helping to bring a tiny bit of warmth to people's day, even helping them out of a negative state. It gave life a bit more meaning for him.

He'd started doing it after suffering with depression. He found that helping other people was a help for him too. Then he realized that just smiling at people achieved a lot as well.

'You have to be genuine though,' he said. 'I think people sense genuine. If you're not, then some people probably will think you're weird. Or you're up to something. And most people do smile back. In fact, everyone smiles back, even if they don't realize they're doing it.'

Studies shows that it's automatic. Volunteers in a study at Uppsala University in Sweden were once asked to sit in front of a screen. It was blank. When asked if they saw anything, they all said no.

Except that the scientists had put a smiling face on the screen, but only for a few thousandths of a second, just faster than the conscious mind can acknowledge – subliminal.

The volunteers were all wearing tiny devices that measured activation of the muscles that control their zygomaticus major muscles. (These are the ones that pull your lips into a smile.) And everyone's zygomaticus major tweaked. They all smiled. It was a fast, almost imperceptible smile, a twitch some might say, but it was a twitch of the smile muscles and in response to perceiving a smile.

We can't even overrule this automatic response with a frown. Some people may try to and then think they've shown you how pissed they are at your smug smile. But they'll smile before they frown.

In another experiment, volunteers were shown facial expressions of someone either smiling or frowning. The same devices were attached to their faces. They were instructed to either not respond to the facial expressions, or to respond oppositely and to frown as soon as they saw a smile, for example.

The result was that we simply can't resist a smile.

When the volunteers were shown a smiling face and tried either to do nothing or to frown, their smile muscles twitched first – *before* their conscious minds could overrule it with a frown.

So if ever you smile at someone and they don't smile back or they give you a 'What are you staring at me for with that smug smile on your face?' look, take comfort from the fact that they really did smile first. They just don't know it.

4

The opposite of stress

Let's start with a quiz! What comes to mind when I say 'opposite of stress'? I bet you're thinking peace, calm, or maybe chill vibes. That's what most people jump to. But here's an interesting twist: That's not the opposite of stress; that's the absence of stress. The true opposite of stress is kindness.

I know, I know – stress is a feeling, but kindness is an action, so how does that work? Stick with me here. Remember when I talked about those feel-good kindness hormones versus the stressy ones? It's all about how stuff actually feels. Let me put it another way: The opposite of the experience of stress, and what that feels like, is the experience of kindness and what that feels like.

There was a study where psychologists sent people a daily text asking for two scores: their stress level (on a scale of 1 to 10) and the approximate number of kind things they did. After a few weeks of data crunching, they found that on days when the participants' kindness number score was high, their stress number score was low. And on days when the stress score was high, the kindness score was low. It was a total seesaw action of opposites – when one went up, the other came down.

Let me say, though, that just because you're being extra kind one day doesn't mean that stressful stuff won't happen. Shit happens, as we all know. One of life's specialties is curveballs and they can fly towards you regardless of how kind you're being. But the silver lining in the cloud of the study data was that if shit does happen, the feelings induced through the experience of kindness can take some of the stink out of it.

In short, kindness is like life's secret sauce, which sweetens stressful circumstances. It won't make problems vanish, but it's like a cushion for your mind when everything feels like a wild river ride. It helps build resilience in the face of stress. It reduces the mental and emotional impact of some stressful events – enough that it might serve up some extra protection for our mental health on those days when life feels like we're swimming upstream against a strong current. And especially on those days when just one more problem might tip us over the edge.

On a chemical level, this is partly due to our warm and fuzzy kindness hormone, oxytocin. Just as the experience of stress produces stress hormones such as adrenalin and cortisol, so the experience of kindness produces kindness hormones.

As well as being a kindness hormone, oxytocin goes by a number of other affectionate names that you may recognize: *the love drug, the hug drug, the cuddle chemical, the bonding hormone*. But the fascinating part is that oxytocin dials down regions of the brain associated with stress, such as the amygdala. Think of it as a dimmer switch: The experience of stress turns the amygdala up, but the experience of kindness, via the action of oxytocin, turns it down. Opposites!

In one piece of research in this area, scientists induced a state of stress in volunteers while they were inside an MRI scanner, and activity in the amygdala shot up. But if they gave them a squirt of kindness hormone up the nose first, before the stress, then the amygdala activity didn't reach anywhere close to those highs. The kindness hormone protected the volunteers against stress at a neurological level. (In case you were wondering about the squirt-up-the-nose thing, it helps the oxytocin to travel across the blood-brain barrier. That's a barrier between the brain and body which helps to block stuff like bacteria and viruses from getting into the brain. But the bouncers at the door will let our kindness hormone in.)

When we feel stressed about something, the usual thing we try to do is relax. Take some slow breaths. And yes, absolutely, do that! But you can go a wee bit further now. If you're feeling stressed, try kindness.

See if you can reach for a few kind thoughts. Who has shown up for you recently or in the past? Who have you helped and in what way? Think of the kindest person you know. What is particularly kind about this person? Or go out and be kind. Do you know anyone who could do with a kind listening ear or a helping hand? You could also try the kindfulness meditation practices in Appendix II, where the focus is on compassion and kindness.

Kindfulness activities like these can change the brain organically in a similar way to the effects of mindfulness; just the regions impacted are different. Kindfulness meditation pumps up regions of the brain – such as the medial prefrontal cortex – which help with the experience of positive emotion and happiness. As these regions become more powerful, extracting happiness and joy from the everyday moments of life becomes a bit easier.

This doesn't mean that you will be instantly and always happy, just that happiness becomes a wee bit more accessible because this part of the brain has had some training. It's like how running 5k in under 40 minutes becomes a little more accessible if you build muscle endurance through training.

Staying with the organic changes in the brain thing, kindfulness practices also pump up empathy regions of the brain (for example, the insula), making it easier to feel empathy for others who are suffering or struggling.

Kindness is your secret sauce in life's apple pie and the ultimate antidote to stress. But, of course, your heart needs to be in the right place, so to speak. That's a phrase I learned as a child – about doing things for the right reasons.

This is where Nature's catch-22 comes in.

Nature's catch-22

This is what I call the glitch in the system. You'll recall how I said earlier that kindness hormones were produced only if kindness was genuine. Think about it. You need to create kindness hormones to get a positive side effect from kindness, and these are produced by how the experience feels. You have to *feel* it.

And you only feel it when you mean it.

That's Nature's catch-22: You only get the benefits of kindness if you mean it, if you're genuine. It's as if Nature has built this into life's equation. If you mean it, you'll feel it, and you'll then get the anti-stress boost plus loads of other healthy benefits.

So be aware that kindness can bring benefits to your mental health, but there's an important caveat: It has to be genuine kindness.

Kindness gives you a younger brain... and face

Most people know that stress speeds up aging, but maybe haven't ever thought about what kindness does. Yep, it's that seesaw of opposites again: The experience of kindness can even slow the rate your brain ages.

Researchers at the University of Wisconsin–Madison and Harvard Medical School once compared the brain of a Tibetan Buddhist monk with people in the general population. These monks do kindfulness and mindfulness meditations every day and follow the Eightfold Path, which roots their thoughts, words, and actions in compassion and kindness. Rumor was that they always seemed to be happy and to defy normal aging.

The researchers took scans of the monk's brain four times over a 14-year period and they compared them with the brain scans of 105 people in the general population aged between 25 and 66. The scans of these 105 people allowed the researchers to get a picture of what an aging brain looks like.

They found that while the monk was 41 years of age, the biological age of his brain was only 33 – eight years younger! His brain was aging much slower than that of the everyday normal person. The reason they found for the slower aging was his intensive meditation practice, which involved both mindfulness and kindfulness.

Another study took the aging thing a bit further and looked at the end caps on DNA. They're called telomeres and they're the DNA version of your shoelace aglets (those plastic bits on the end). Both telomeres and aglets wear down under stress. In fact, measuring the length of your telomeres and how fast they wear down is one of the most accurate ways of calculating biological age.

In the research, volunteers either practiced mindfulness or kindfulness every day for six weeks and the length of their telomeres was compared against people who weren't doing either. The researchers discovered that mindfulness slowed the rate of decline in the length of telomeres by just a little, but kindfulness stopped it altogether.

Of course, this doesn't mean that kindfulness will stop you aging. Mind you, I've been practicing it daily for going on 127 years now and I'm told I don't look a day over 126. But seriously, this was a single study for a relatively small duration of time and it only measured one thing – telomere length. However, it does tell us that the experience of kindness can impact upon aging in our cells in some pretty amazing and heavy-duty ways. Among other things, this is probably what was going on in the brain cells of the Tibetan Buddhist monk who practiced kindfulness every day for years.

If that weren't enough, scientists did a study on skin cells. They put the cells under stress in the lab in a way that was meant to simulate the stresses our skin feels from too much UV light, the diets we consume, and from the mental and emotional stresses we go through.

Then they examined what happened to the skin cells. One thing was a big elevation in free radicals – substances that play a key role in aging, heart disease, memory loss, dementia, and a whole heap of age-related conditions.

Stress increases free radicals in the skin. Noted. But then they repeated the process in the presence of oxytocin – the kindness hormone I spoke of earlier. Now, amazingly, the levels of free radicals were way less. Kindness hormones counteract some of the effects of aging in our skin.

Here's the thing – you can't eat or drink kindness hormones. You can't buy them in supplement form, nor make juices out of them. You can't put them in face creams or oils. They can only be created inside the brain and body.

And one of the ways to do this is to be kind, and to be genuine about it.

Lead from the heart and it's good for your immune system

Chronic stress isn't exactly a friend to our immune system. It can really knock it down a peg. Some researchers started thinking that perhaps being kind has something to do with keeping our immune system in tip-top shape, helping us fend off illness. To put this idea to the test, they measured how kindness affected certain immune system genes (known as CTRA) in 159 adults.

They found that when people were kind toward others, there were key changes in the activity of the genes: Kindness not only impacts our cells, but also has genetic effects in anti-aging ways!

Other researchers asked volunteers to watch an inspiring film with scenes showing displays of compassion and kindness. They took before and after levels of an immune system antibody and found that just watching the film boosted them by around 50 percent. The boost stayed up for hours afterward because the volunteers kept reminiscing about specific scenes that had moved them. Even recalling kindness was having an immune-boosting, anti-aging effect.

A kind heart is a happy heart

It's pretty well known these days that stress can increase blood pressure. What isn't so well known is how kindness can lower blood pressure.

The study in Chapter 3 showed how people's happiness was increased if they spent money on others rather than on themselves. Researchers decided to do a similar study with older adults. Only now they weren't measuring happiness; they were measuring blood pressure.

The participants were asked to spend money on others or spend money on themselves for three weeks. After this time, those who had spent money on others had lower systolic and diastolic blood pressure than those asked to spend money on themselves. Amazingly, the magnitude of the effect was as strong as the effect of taking antihypertensive medication or exercise.

A lot of this is down to our kindness hormones. They park on the lining of our blood vessels. OK, so when I say park, I mean 'bind to receptors' there. That's the pharmacological term, but as binding is basically the same as parking, let's go with parking from here on in.

There are loads of parking bays in cells all throughout the brain and body. They're similar in some ways to the ones in big car parks, like at motorway services. There are bays for buses and caravans, smaller ones for SUVs, average-sized ones for standard-sized cars, and even small, thin ones for motorcycles. Each vehicle will only fit snugly in its own bay.

In blood vessels, there are also vehicles and parking bays, except that the vehicles are hormones and the parking bays are our receptor binding sites. And many of the ones that line blood vessels are an exact fit for our kindness hormone. They're actually called 'oxytocin receptors;' i.e., kindness hormone receptors. When we have an experience of kindness and it triggers the release of kindness hormones, they park in these bays.

Then some cool biology happens that basically results in the production of nitric oxide (not nit*rous* oxide; that's laughing gas). Nitric oxide is the substance that Viagra helps pump up.

There's also ANP – atrial natriuretic peptide. Between the two of them – ANP but mostly nitric oxide – blood vessel walls relax and expand (or dilate, if we want to use the proper term). Now, with a wider blood vessel, the heart doesn't need to work as hard to push blood through, so it eases off some of its pressure. What we get from this is a reduction in blood pressure.

That's how kindness hormones reduce blood pressure and thus also partly how an experience of kindness, whether you're the giver, receiver, or witness to it, can lower blood pressure. I say partly because kindness also relaxes the nervous system and that lowers blood pressure too. It's a win–win!

If you've ever wondered why kindness not only feels good, but sometimes gives us that nice, warm feeling in the chest, this is why: an increase in blood flow to the heart from more relaxed and wider blood vessels.

It's also why mothers tend to have lower blood pressure while nursing their young. In fact, that's where all this research into the blood-pressure-lowering effects of oxytocin started. Scientists were curious as to why it was and how it worked. It wasn't long before they identified oxytocin's effect on blood vessels and all the parking and stuff.

Due to this effect and a few others, oxytocin is known as a *cardioprotective hormone*. That is, it protects the cardiovascular system. That means kindness is cardioprotective. Incredible! Just as chronic stress can damage the cardiovascular system, it means that kindness protects it. Opposites again!

Taking out the garbage

Kindness hormones also help clear the garbage out of blood vessels – which brings us back to free radicals, those things that play a big role in aging. Free radicals get produced in blood vessels in response to stress – along with inflammation, which is what happens when you get a cut and it begins to heal, for example.

Free radicals and inflammation rise on the inside of our bodies when we experience stress over a period of time. It doesn't matter whether it's because you're stressed at work, pissed because someone took your parking space, you're eating highly processed foods every day, or even lying in the sun way much longer than you should – it's stress, all the same.

Free radicals and inflammation are in large part responsible for a lot of the damage that stress does to the brain and body. They're what happens on the inside as you experience some of the world that's on the outside.

But here's the magic. Kindness is the opposite of stress, so we can guess what kindness hormones do to free radicals and inflammation.... Yep! Sweep them out with the garbage.

Experiments on cells from blood vessel walls and on some immune cells has shown that oxytocin acts as an antioxidant (meaning it neutralizes free radicals) and an anti-inflammatory (in that it neutralizes inflammation, like your body's own version of ibuprofen, only better). And it does this in both blood vessels and some parts of the immune system.

So while stress can create free radicals and inflammation, kindness can eliminate them through the action of kindness hormones. Opposites!

A summary

Isn't it amazing that kindness is the opposite of stress – psychologically, neurologically, and physiologically? Just like a grown-up gave you a sweet for being good as a child, it's Nature's reward for being good as an adult.

Of all the shit that happens in the body as a consequence of stress, kindness sweeps much of it up and puts it in the trash.

Kindness calms the mind and creates a warm feeling where stress feels like crap.

Kindness lowers blood pressure where stress feels like your blood is boiling.

Kindness slows aging while stress accelerates it.

Kindness makes your skin smoother and younger where stress can make us look, yep, stressed.

Kindness can improve immune function where stress can suppress it.

Even in relationships, kindness can bring peace where stress tends to escalate conflicts.

And the same for a lot of other things you can think of that scientists haven't even got around to testing yet. You can pretty much bet that whatever stress does, kindness does the opposite.

Most heroes
don't wear capes

Nicholas Winton was a British stockbroker. In 1939, he learned about the deteriorating situation in Czechoslovakia, as Hitler was expanding his influence. Worried about Jewish children at risk of persecution, Nicholas began organizing a rescue operation.

He worked tirelessly, coordinating with parents and refugee organizations to arrange for children to be transported safely to Britain. He found foster families, organized paperwork, secured the necessary travel documents. And he found a way to arrange for eight trains to carry 669 children from Prague to London. Just in time too, because the last train he organized left on the very same day that Germany invaded Poland.

Nicholas Winton was a hero, though his efforts were initially overshadowed by the outbreak of World War II and his work remained mostly forgotten for decades. That was until 1988 – when his wife found a scrapbook in their attic in Maidenhead, near London. It had records of the rescue operation. And it led to the discovery of the children he had saved.

That's Life was a TV show in the UK in the 1980s. In one episode, Nicholas and his wife were invited onto the show. Nicholas was now 78 years old. Esther Rantzen, the show's presenter, brought the camera over to him. She relayed to viewers what he had done back in 1939. And then she said, 'Is there anyone in the audience today who owes their life to Nicholas Winton?'

Virtually the whole studio audience stood up. The show had tracked many of them down and arranged for them to be there that day... to say thank you to the man who saved their lives all those years ago. He gazed around and met their eyes as they looked upon him with deep, loving affection. It was one of the most heart-warming moments in British TV, watched by millions of viewers.

It helped bring his heroic actions to the forefront of public attention. He later received an MBE and a knighthood, becoming Sir Nicholas Winton. He died on July 1, 2015 at the age of 106 – but not before the Czech Republic had awarded him their highest honor, the Order of the White Lion (first class).

He once said of his actions, 'Anything that is not actually impossible can be done, if one really sets one's mind to it and is determined that it shall be done.' And if your actions are fueled with kindness, miracles can be made to happen.

Yet while his were actions of extraordinary heroism, please don't think that an ordinary person can't be a hero too. We can't all be Nicholas Wintons or Oscar Schindlers. In fact, heroism is all around us in ways we barely recognize. Sometimes, it's in the seemingly small and mundane acts that lifelong memories are forged, like when a parent becomes a hero to their children just through comforting them if they cut a finger or graze a knee.

The belief that kindness needs to be visibly heroic makes many of us feel inadequate, as if something has to be visible to count as kind. But the everyday, ordinary kindnesses matter because these are the things we do every day. These, in fact, are the stitches in the very fabric of human society. Listening to someone – a friend or family member – who wants to talk helps them feel validated. Holding a door. Picking up a dropped object. Offering a reassuring smile or a gentle squeeze on the shoulder that says, 'You've got this! And if by chance you haven't then I've got *you!*'

It's the parents who work two jobs to give their kids a better life. It's the people who foster or adopt babies and children. It's the friend who drops what they're doing and is immediately there for someone who has had a row with a partner and feels like life is over. It's the housemate who turns away from a favorite TV show because their roomie has arrived home and needs to offload about work. It's a kind word when someone needs it – and even when they don't.

These sorts of things will never make the news. Not even a social media post. Often, no one even notices. But these are the acts of the people who hold our world together. Not the governments. Not the business leaders. Not the tech entrepreneurs. It's about the people who would call themselves ordinary; the people who are kind every day just because it's in their nature.

There's much more to heroism than demonstrating great strength or courage in the face of immense (often life-threatening) adversity. It's not about being Wonder Woman, Superman, or some other super character we see in movies. In real life, heroism extends far beyond physical strength and courage.

In real life, it's in simple everyday acts of kindness.

The biology of heroism

My dad passed away a few months before I began working on this book. He had a brain tumor – glioblastoma multiforme. His health suddenly declined in the last few months of his life. Mum just stepped up. No complaints.

She once told me that it was her job to look after Dad. She put aside all the things she usually did for herself. Her weekly bingo with friends. Sunday tea with her sister Jane after church. The occasional night out with former work friends. My sisters and I did the best we could to help her still do some of those things, but the way the tumor affected Dad in the last few months left him anxious when Mum wasn't there. So my sisters and I organized more support. The district nurse got involved, and MacMillan Cancer support came in twice a day.

I still don't know how Mum managed to get him to the bathroom in the middle of the night. He was 14 stone (89kg), in part due to the steroids he was having to take to stem some of the inflammation in his brain, and he had little strength left in his legs or arms. Mum was 77 years old at the time. I stayed over for a few nights, and it took both of us almost an hour to help him to the bathroom and back. Yet Mum just did what she did. No complaints.

Mum is a hero to me and showed heroism throughout Dad's illness, as do many people who are at-home caregivers. Most people are unaware of how many people care for family members full time, putting their own lives on hold as they silently take on a life-changing role.

The point I'm making is that most heroes don't wear capes. Our friend empathy is often where heroism begins. There's something instinctual. A knowing. We can see the spark in the brain, literally. Brain imaging studies reveal activation in empathy regions when a person acts heroically.

Even witnessing someone in pain activates brain regions in the observer as if they themselves were in pain. Seeing someone suffer touches us deeply. It's as if the brain isn't distinguishing between us and the person we care about; it's as if we're one.

Besides empathy being a motivator of some acts of heroism, there are many consequences, or side effects, of heroism, not just for the person helped, but for the helper too.

The kindness (heroism) hormone

Here's a bit more about our kindness hormone, oxytocin, and why it's also a heroism hormone. It was discovered by the British pharmacologist and physiologist Sir Henry Dale in 1906. The name he gave it derives from Greek and means 'swift birth.' This is because it's mostly released abundantly during labor, but it participates in a wide range of other stuff too, including lactation, orgasm, social bonding, maternal behaviors, cardiovascular health, and much more. Women produce it not only when they're with their babies but even when they're apart from them and are just thinking about their babies.

It is abundantly produced in response to empathy and many forms of kindness. Paul Zak, a leader in oxytocin–empathy connection research, wrote, 'I now consider oxytocin the neurologic substrate for the Golden Rule: If you treat me well, in most cases my brain will synthesize oxytocin and this will motivate me to treat you well in return.'

One study to demonstrate this found that oxytocin was produced abundantly in the brains of people who watched a video where a father stayed close to his son until the very end as the son died of cancer. Yet when another group watched an emotionally flat video clip instead, their brains didn't produce any oxytocin at all.

If you lead with your heart, it's good for your heart

Kindness and heroism bring about effects all through the body. This is because changes in brain oxytocin are reflected in changes in blood oxytocin.

As I wrote in the previous chapter, oxytocin is a 'cardioprotective' hormone and it causes the release of nitric oxide and atrial natriuretic peptide. The production of nitric oxide is key.

Nitric oxide is one of oxytocin's work buddies; they hang out quite a bit and do a load of stuff together. It's also one of the most important molecules in the body. Back in 1992, it was actually nicknamed 'Molecule of the Year,' a kind of science-geek version of *Time*'s 'Person of the Year.' In fact, the 1998 Nobel Prize in Physiology or Medicine was awarded for the discovery of its role in the cardiovascular system. One of the brains who received the prize, Dr. Louis J. Ignarro, even calls it the 'Miracle Molecule.' It's a cardiac superhero as it plays a massive role in maintaining the health of the heart and arteries. It's like the body's natural relaxer – and one of the things it relaxes is the smooth muscles in blood vessel walls.

This is how kindness reduces blood pressure.

As we learned earlier, an experience of kindness produces kindness hormones (oxytocin). This then kicks nitric oxide into action, which relaxes the smooth muscles in blood vessel walls, and so blood pressure comes down.

And it's not just about the heart. The oxytocin–nitric oxide partnership (also known as oxytocin-induced nitric oxide release) helps relax the smooth muscles in the uterine walls when it's time for childbirth and makes sure blood flows well in the reproductive organs.

In simple terms, for our cardiovascular system, nitric oxide enables things to flow smoothly, helps manage our blood pressure, and keeps our blood vessels in tip-top shape to support overall cardiovascular function.

All of this is also why the simple heroic act of supporting a loved one – and yes, that counts as heroism – not only produces oxytocin but reduces blood pressure. Researchers have now shown that giving loving emotional support to a partner or just giving someone a hug produces oxytocin. Oxytocin then gives nitric oxide a nudge and both the emotional heart and the physical heart relax.

We saw earlier how oxytocin does its antioxidant and anti-inflammatory thing with vascular and immune cells, where levels of oxidative stress (free radicals) and inflammation drop dramatically.

Oxidative stress is the chemical version of mental and emotional stress. It's when the body's natural defense processes can't cope with the amount of free radicals being produced in the body. So the free radicals have a field day. They run riot and do whatever they want. They cause damage to blood vessels, immune cells, tissue cells, skin, and even in the brain, where this then contributes to memory loss and dementia. They also play a significant role in aging.

Here's a fun fact about free radicals: They are like atoms that used to be in a relationship but are now single. The oxygen gas that we breathe is composed of two oxygen atoms connected by a bond – a bit like a pair of spectacles, where the bit over your nose is the bond. Sometimes, that bond gets broken, not just in oxygen, but in other different types of molecules in the body. Two atoms that were once connected are now separated. This is what a free radical is: an atom that was previously in a relationship but is now single.

Only it hates being single. Free radicals are so desperate to reconnect, to get back into a relationship, that they will try to covet an atom from some other seemingly stable relationship (which in chemical terms is a group of atoms, aka a molecule). If it happens to be a molecule that supports brain cells, then free radicals can lead to memory loss. If it's in the heart, this can lead to heart disease. I think you get the picture.

The natural antidote to free radicals is antioxidants. Antioxidants provide a willing partner to free radicals. Once the antioxidants arrive on the scene, the poor things are no longer single and can now enjoy a happy new chapter in their lives. They stop wreaking havoc and the body returns to peace.

This is one of the reasons that antioxidant-laden fruits and vegetables are so good for the heart and why antioxidants are added to beauty products.

Crucially, oxytocin – our kindness and heroism hormone – acts as an antioxidant (and an anti-inflammatory) in blood vessels, the immune system, and throughout the body, even in skin cells, as we saw earlier. And in this way, it helps to protect cells from damage.

We can actually boost the levels of oxytocin in our skin. Have you ever noticed how your skin has an extra glow after intimate moments? That's oxytocin at work. It triggers the release of nitric oxide, which gets the blood pumping more to your skin, lighting up your face with that special sparkle. But oxytocin goes beyond making skin glow: It helps to keep our skin young. Not just young-looking, but actually young, by neutralizing the effect of free radicals.

And there's more. Oxytocin isn't just about healthy skin; it also plays a big part in keeping muscles strong and helps them heal after a workout or injury. It does this for our heart's muscles, too.

It's even involved in the growth of the heart from the time we're tiny babies. Oxytocin prohormones (these are substances that the body converts into oxytocin) kick-start the conversion of stem cells into heart muscle cells and then into fully functional contracting heart muscle. It's also a behind-the-scenes hero that helps us digest food by assisting the muscular contractions that move food through the gut. It even helps facilitate wound healing. Phew! Science binge! But I thought you'd appreciate the full rundown on how incredible this kindness hormone is.

So oxytocin does a lot of things. It's kind of a big deal. And it doesn't wear a cape either. What's more, many acts of kindness and heroism produce it. This tells us that all these healthy things can in some way be pumped up by kindness and other acts of heroism.

This shouldn't come as too much of a surprise, given that we know all of these things are negatively affected by stress. Kindness is the opposite of stress, after all. If stress hampers all these processes, which we know it does, then it makes sense that kindness and heroism should counteract the processes.

There are real, true, deep and powerful biological effects that occur when you're kind. They're Nature's reward for being a decent person. That's not why we're kind. We help each other because doing so is the right thing to do. But Nature rewards us all the same. And this is how.

Adults in Making

The Adults in Making (AIM) program is an initiative that helps young people navigate the challenges of life. We all know that growing up can be tough, so the goal of AIM is to offer a comforting hand – be it through emotional chats, helpful skill-building sessions, mental health support, or just fostering strong friendships. It's about making sure young people have solid connections in their lives, both at home and in their neighborhoods. Kindness is there at every stage.

Parents are involved too. AIM guides them on how to be there for their kids, listen to their concerns, and become their pillars of strength. It's like creating a village of love and care.

Here's the mind-blowing part: There was a study of 17-year-olds in the AIM program which looked at their telomeres, those tiny DNA endcaps that act like our body's biological clock, ticking away as we age. When life gets tough, they can wear down faster than they should, which isn't great for our health. Yet after five years in AIM, the teens had noticeably longer telomeres compared to others their age who weren't in the program. It's like AIM somehow tapped into the secret for keeping our biological clocks in check!

It really goes to show how critical it is to have support early on. When young people feel understood and cherished, it doesn't just lift their spirits – it might just keep them biologically younger too!

Kindness to animals

When I think of kindness, I include animals. I've always loved them. Like many kids growing up, I had a goldfish and a hamster. We also had a dog named Sam and two cats – Buttons and Sooty. But I had a significant moment as an adult after we lost our dog, Oscar, in 2014. At just two years old, he had bone cancer and we'd done everything we could to try to save his life.

Caring for a sick animal does something to you. It intensified the bond we had with him in a way I didn't know was possible. When he died, it burst me right open. A month or two later, I was driving through the countryside to speak at a retreat when I stopped at a coffee shop by the side of the road. As I parked my car, I saw a large shaggy-haired Highland cow. They're popular in Scotland.

It wandered over to the fence where I'd parked. As I got out of the car, I came face to face with it. It had an enormous head and I found myself staring into its huge, deep, dark eyes. And then I saw it! I mean, I really *saw* it.

I found myself crumpling to the ground. I burst into tears. It was the first time, outside of my experience with Oscar, that I'd truly considered that animals have emotional lives, personalities. It was alive with life itself. Pure. Vibrant. That's the only way I can describe it. A real conscious being with feelings. In that moment, I knew it could experience happiness and sadness. I could tell it was playful. It felt!

I know this is obvious to many people, but sometimes you need to have a powerful, soul-stirring experience to really grasp the profoundly important things in life. It changed a lot of things for me. I have also never eaten meat since that moment.

Nature loves all her creations. She rewards kindness to animals just as much as she rewards kindness to humans. She rewards kindness, regardless of who or what we show kindness too.

Being kind to animals produces oxytocin in volumes. In a study that measured the quality of interaction with a dog, good-quality interaction for half an hour produced more than three times more oxytocin in the human (and 1.5 times more in the dog) than normal.

That's about an increase of 10 percent per minute over the half hour! Now, 10 percent in total would have been impressive enough, given that oxytocin is a cardio-protective hormone, but 10 percent per minute is something else entirely.

This may explain the observation that the chances of a second heart attack within one year in people who have already had one is significantly lower if they have a dog in their family. In fact, some research suggests it's as much as 400 percent lower.

The peak in oxytocin consistently through the day as a person interacts warmly, lovingly, kindly, and playfully with the dog helps control blood pressure, reduce oxidative stress, and reduce inflammation, rendering some healthier conditions for the heart.

Of course, some of the effect will also come from taking the dog for a walk. But in saying this I don't want to play down the importance of the relationship with the dog in any way. This is because large studies that look at the effects of having not only dogs, but cats or rabbits in the family – in other words, animals that we tend to bond with – show that the bonds we develop help protect us from heart attack and stroke.

The strength of the effect in cats and dogs is more or less the same. Now, given that we don't typically take cats for a walk, one might argue that a large part of the protective effect against having a heart attack or a stroke is as much, or possibly more, to do with the *relationship* with the animal as it is from the exercise we get from accompanying it on a walk.

The heroic nerve

Our kindness hormone is strongly correlated with the activity of the vagus nerve. If you're wondering what this is, no, it's not a nerve related to a love of gambling, nor is it the title of the next big sci-fi blockbuster (though that does sound cool). The vagus nerve is actually one of the longest nerves in our body and like a Swiss Army knife of nerves, it does a lot of things. First off, it connects our brain to many of our essential organs, including our heart, lungs, and stomach. So you can think of it as the brain's superhighway for chatting with these organs.

When the vagus nerve is feeling good, it helps to keep our heart rate steady and tells our digestive system to do its thing. It also plays a big role in our 'rest and digest' system – that cozy feeling you get after a big meal when all you want to do is chill on the couch.

And that's not all – the vagus nerve is also linked to our emotions and how we handle stress. Ever had a gut feeling, or felt your heart race when you're nervous? Well, you can thank (or sometimes blame) the vagus nerve for that. It's like that behind-the-scenes crew member in a movie – it might not always be in the spotlight, but boy, does it play a crucial role in making sure everything runs smoothly.

The vagus nerve is strongly correlated with empathy and compassion. It isn't just a highway between the brain and various organs; it's also deeply involved in our social-emotional lives. One of its standout roles is in the 'social engagement system,' a fancy term for how we connect, communicate, and bond with others.

Here's the lowdown on how that works. The vagus nerve helps regulate facial muscles and vocalizations. When you see someone in distress and your eyebrows furrow in empathy or your voice takes on a soothing tone, that's the vagus nerve working its magic. By facilitating these expressions, it plays a role in our ability to show compassion to others.

When we feel compassion for someone, our heart rate may decrease, and our breathing can become deeper and more regular. These responses are mediated by the vagus nerve powering up. If you've ever felt that warm, expansive feeling in your chest when moved by compassion, yep, as well as oxytocin, that's our friend the vagus nerve making its presence known.

High vagal tone (a measure of the health and activity of the vagus nerve) is associated with the ability to regulate our emotions and with feeling safer in social situations. When we feel safe and secure, we are more likely to open up, connect with others, and exhibit compassionate behaviors.

Some kindfulness meditation practices (like metta, a Buddhist loving-kindness meditation, which you'll find in Appendix II), that involve producing a feeling of compassion for someone and wishing them relief from suffering, have also been shown to increase vagal tone, as well as to reduce the inflammatory response to stress.

Kevin Tracy proposed the existence of 'the inflammatory reflex' in 2002, when he showed that the vagus nerve controls inflammation. It does this by turning down, like you would a dimmer switch, a gene for inflammation (TNF-alpha).

Vagus nerve activity even has effects on cancer prognosis due to its anti-inflammatory ability. In some research, stage-4 cancer patients with high vagus nerve activity were found to live much longer than patients with low activity. In fact, in a statistical analysis of such studies, researchers wrote that the anti-inflammatory effect of high vagus nerve activity was benefiting stage-4 patients even at a stage when medication was less effective.

Given that compassion, kindness, and heroism can increase vagus nerve activity, it may be that compassion, kindness, and heroism (or even just a generally kind attitude) could have extra important anti-inflammatory effects and overall beneficial health consequences.

Of course, this doesn't mean that being kind guarantees good health. Common sense tells us that this isn't true. We all know kind people who got sick and nasty people who lived a long life. But, with all things being equal, without doubt a kind attitude could certainly make us healthier than an unkind one – in body as well as in mind. But not everything is equal in life, which is why it's not always clear-cut when drawing conclusions.

Be kind anyway. It's almost certainly doing you, and others, a lot of good.

Mindfully kind

Let's chat about life for moment. You know how sometimes you think you've got someone all figured out based on their Instagram, or the way they always nail that perfect coffee order?

Well, here's a reality check: Everyone's got their stuff. That's why the mantra 'be kind because you never know what someone is going through' isn't just a trendy T-shirt design or a cute quote for a wall print – it's genuinely golden advice.

Think of people as being a bit like books. And I don't mean the kind that are judged by their covers (even though we're all guilty of that sometimes). I mean that every person has a story filled with twisty plot points, heartwarming moments, and some chapters they might want to skip. While one person might be dealing with a tricky past, another could be juggling present-day dramas. Even if someone's life looks like a fairy tale from the outside, remember: Fairy tales often have dungeons.

The fact is that most of us are basically like award-winning actors when it comes to hiding our real emotions. Maybe it's society, maybe it's pride, but many of us put on a brave face even when we're feeling anything but brave inside. That super-cheerful coworker? Maybe they're having tough nights. Your always-there-for-you friend? They might need someone to be there for them, too.

If we all just started being a bit kinder, pausing for a moment to imagine the little battles everyone's fighting, the world might be a friendlier place. Fewer mean tweets, more 'you got this' vibes.

Everyone's dealing with something. Everyone's fighting their own battles, and some in silence. So, if we lean into kindness, it not only makes someone's day a bit brighter, it makes the world feel a little smaller and a lot cozier. And we could all use a bit more of that.

You never know what someone is dealing with

I was running late one morning while driving to collect Mum and Dad so that we could drive the 38 miles (60km) to one of Dad's radiotherapy treatments. It was a series of events. You know what it's like. Despite the best will in the world, stuff happens.

Dad would get anxious if he wasn't early. In fact, if I was picking them up at 9 a.m., Dad would be sitting in the living room an hour earlier with his jacket and hat on. It was the way the tumor affected his brain.

I wasn't exactly late, but late enough that we might not get there 30 to 40 minutes early. And being at least 30 minutes early was important to Dad. I felt disappointed in myself.

With so much on my mind, the worry of being late combined with the reality of Dad's condition, my attention wasn't fully on my driving. Close to their home, I pulled onto a mini roundabout right in front of another car. We both rammed on our brakes. There was almost a crash – and it was totally my fault.

But the other driver just smiled and waved me on. It was a kind, warm smile, too. His open hand gesture said, 'It's OK. On you go!' I smiled back and waved my hand.

I burst into tears a hundred yards or so along the road. I had expected him to slam his hand on his horn and belt out some expletives at me. After all, isn't that what seems to happen so often on roads these days?

I couldn't have coped with that. Not today. Despite the front I showed to the world, to the readers of my books, audiences at my talks, the viewers of my social media videos, I was fragile inside.

The driver showed me kindness. It was almost too much. That's why I got emotional. The stress of being potentially late melted in an instant. The anxiety about Dad's condition was momentarily gone, or at least softened by that act of kindness. To this day, the driver who waved me on at the roundabout has no idea about the consequences of his action. He had no idea what it meant to me, what I was going through.

That's how kindness works. You never know what's happening in a person's life. And you rarely know how much your kindness means to them.

OK, not everyone is suffering. I get that. Some people, for whatever reason, act selfishly a lot. But that doesn't mean we need to lead with the assumption that *everyone* is selfish or has hostile intentions – just so some people don't 'get away with it.' That way of thinking punishes the well-meaning people who really are working through a heavy chapter in the book of their life and yet, as we all do, they are trying to put on a brave face to get through one day at a time.

We can't know. The way I see it, then, is that we may as well be kind and take the higher ground.

Given the statistics, it's probably the case that lots of people you encounter each day *are* struggling in some way, despite the face they show to the world. A 2023 survey of 30,000 people in 16 countries, for example, found that while 23 percent of people felt they were flourishing, 35 percent felt they were just 'getting by,' 28 percent felt they were languishing, and 13 percent said they were struggling.

If we have been treated unfairly ourselves and then perpetuate this by passing on that treatment to another person, we create a downward spiral. The compulsion to treat others badly because we've been treated badly has to stop somewhere.

I understand. Life sucks sometimes. Sometimes a lot. But when it does, maybe we can help make it suck a little less for someone else. After all, we know what it feels like.

You don't need to put someone down so you can win

The world can sometimes seem like a roller coaster with all its ups and downs – and kindness doesn't always seem like the best route to the stability of peace and happiness. Which may be why some people don't let kindness in. But I'd say that this is usually more to do with our general lack of experience in trying a kind approach.

You see, while experience teaches us that kindness can be transformational, the trouble is we're not set many good public examples. What we do often see and read about are squabbling politicians, celebrity gossip, and negative news – all at the expense of the examples of love and kindness that happen every day all over the world. And seriously, doesn't it sometimes seem like everyone's just ready to jump into 'outrage mode' at a drop of a hat?

I genuinely believe a few drops of kindness here and there can make a world of difference. Maybe, before joining the mass critique of that celebrity or politician, we can just take a sec. Put ourselves in their shoes. Think about how we'd react if we were facing the same pressures.

Now, I'm not saying we give everyone a free pass or turn a blind eye to mistakes. But what I am saying is there's a difference between going 'OMG, what on earth were they thinking?!' and just outright vicious name-calling and canceling.

When there's a political debate on TV, some people get so heated, it's almost like watching a schoolyard brawl. It's like, 'Come on, you guys probably played nicer in the sandbox!'

Every time I see a negative ad against a politician, even if I'm not a fan, it bums me out. Surely there's a better way to shine, without dimming someone else's light, right? And surely there's a better example we can set our kids.

Because disagreeing doesn't mean we have to tear each other down. Instead of shouting, how about saying, 'I get where they're coming from, but here's where I differ.' Keeping it nice. The strength you show in your example of kindness will inspire others to follow suit.

And if someone does go on the offensive? Stand your ground, but do it with class. After all, taking the high road always feels better.

The trouble is that we've learned that we need to win in life and that, to win, kindness often needs to take a back seat. But that's not true at all. You can win in life while being kind.

How do you win while being kind?

OK, let's address how we can win in the game of life without throwing others under the bus. Here are a few thoughts.

1. What's winning anyway?

We need to start by redefining winning. We don't need to view success as defeating others. There's achieving while helping others do so too. We can think of it as reaching the finish line hand in hand with others. Teamwork makes the dream work, as they say – and that dream can be about making the whole world a brighter place.

2. Walk in their shoes

Practice empathy – try getting a feel for where others are coming from. It makes the journey a lot more fun and a lot less bumpy.

3. Talk the talk

Honesty is golden, but being kind while you're at it – that's platinum. Listen more, chat with heart, and remember that everyone's got a story.

4. Pick your playgrounds

Not every disagreement is a duel at dawn. Sometimes it's cool to agree to disagree and grab a coffee together afterward.

5. Be the gift that keeps on giving

Instead of always asking, 'What's in it for me?', think about how you can sprinkle a bit of joy around. Ask, 'What can I give? How can I help?'

6. Be the change

If you want the world, your place of work, or your community to be kinder, start with yourself. Be the role model for the kindness and integrity you seek. Others will catch on, and before you know it, kindness will be the new black.

7. Friends before trophies

Sure, that gold star is shiny, but the glow of good friendships lasts a lifetime. Winning at the expense of a relationship can be a hollow victory, while maintaining good relationships will create more opportunities in the future.

8. Stick to your guns (but keep them friendly)

It's great to win, but if you're bending your moral compass to get there, you might end up lost. Integrity in the long run is valuable and is respected more than any single achievement.

9. Two winners are better than one

Screw zero-sum thinking (where one person's gain is another person's loss). Look for the solution where everyone gets a slice of the victory pie. Who doesn't love pie?

10. Cheer squad

Be the one who throws confetti when someone else shines. It's fun and there's enough confetti for everyone.

11. Count your blessings

While you're at it, take time to remember all the people who helped you get where you are.

12. Oops! That wasn't right...

Finally, let's remember: We all f*ck up sometimes. Own it, laugh it off, make it right, and keep dancing.

In a nutshell, winning's great, but doing it with a big heart? Now that's the real jackpot in life.

How to explain kindness to kids

I'm going to take a wee sidestep here. One of my books is called *The Little Book of Kindness*. It's meant for adults, but because it's small and filled with colorful illustrations of kindness facts and concepts, loads of kids read it too. I didn't expect that when I wrote it.

Even young kids get their parents to explain the ideas to them.

I've also given a handful of short kindness talks in schools, and parents often ask me how to explain kindness concepts to children. So, here's one of the ways you could explain to kids some of the important reasons for kindness and the benefits of it.

Let's say you have a big box of colorful crayons, and every day at school, you decide to share them with your friends. When you share and are kind, a few things happen:

1. It makes your friends smile

When you're kind, it's like giving a small gift of happiness to someone. If you've ever noticed how people smile when you're nice to them, you'll know it feels good.

2. It makes making friends easier

If you're the kid who is always kind and sharing, more people will want to be around you. Kindness is like a magnet. It attracts others because everyone likes feeling appreciated and cared for.

3. It comes back to you

Kindness is a bit like a boomerang. When you throw a boomerang, it comes back to you. Similarly, when you're kind to others, they're more likely to be kind to you. Maybe one day you'll forget your lunch, and that friend you shared crayons with might offer you half of their sandwich.

4. It makes you feel good

Doing good things for others can make you feel happy inside. It's like when you eat your favorite ice cream or watch a film that makes you laugh. Being kind can give you a warm feeling in your heart, because it creates happy hormones.

5. It makes you healthy

The happy hormones that kindness makes in your body do lots of wonderful things, including making your brain and heart work better, and even help you recover faster when you're sick.

6. It makes the world better

Think about if everyone in the world decided to be just a little bit kinder every day. It would be like turning the world into a big, happy playground where everyone is looking out for each other.

So, being kind is like sharing your crayons. It makes school, or anywhere you go, a brighter and happier place for everyone, including you!

If you want to explain kindness to kids, I hope that helps, even a little.

Healing the emotional heart

Cum Scienta Caritas is the motto of the Royal College of General Practitioners. It means scientific knowledge applied with compassion. Science with heart!

As I said earlier, I lost my dad shortly before I began work on this book. I like to think he had a hand in the idea for me writing it.

Dad was only 78 years old, and very fit, when they found his brain tumor. He and his friend Jake walked almost every day, racking up around 30 to 40 miles (50 to 65km) a week. It was their thing to walk along the Forth and Clyde canal in central Scotland, finishing off with a nice cool pint in a nearby village. Some of the locals in one pub affectionately nicknamed them Jack and Victor, a take on the highly popular Scottish comedy *Still Game*, which centered on the lives of two retired men.

When Dad's leg started giving him some trouble, a scan revealed the 3in (7cm) tumor. We all went with him to see the surgeon – Mum, my three sisters, and myself. The younger surgeons didn't want to risk surgery on Dad, given his age, but Paul Brennan, a consultant neurosurgeon who helped found the Compassionate Initiative at Edinburgh University, stepped up and offered to operate.

He appealed to Dad's pride in his fitness when he looked Dad in the eye and said, 'You're not a normal 78-year-old man.'

The surgery went well, but it wasn't a complete fix, given the location of the tumor. Dad had to go through radiotherapy and chemo. Tough times, but it gave us precious extra moments with him.

Dad never lost his spirit. Even after hearing his prognosis, he was like, 'I've had a good life.' As for me? Honestly, I struggled to keep it together. Those moments were so raw. Even so, I treasure the memories of those days.

I also realized something profound: The kindness and empathy from the doctors and nurses weren't just a nice touch; they were as vital to Dad as the treatment itself. It's amazing how much emotional support can heal. Sometimes in life you need to witness something yourself before the true value of it sinks in.

'My son is a doctor,' he would tell them. I would usually add that my doctorate is in organic chemistry, not medicine. But telling the medical staff always made Dad feel good, and was sometimes how he struck up a conversation. They were all very kind to him. And Dad was a likable man.

Even the little things, like my nephew getting a Band-Aid for a non-bleeding finger after he jammed it in a door, show how much care matters. Once his gran (my mum) put the Band-Aid on, his pain seemed to go away. A doctor friend once told me that letting patients talk is sometimes the best medicine. It's all about connection.

Studies even back this up. Patients with empathetic doctors recover faster or have better outcomes.

Whether it's the common cold or something more serious like cancer, empathy plays a huge role.

Research found that patients with cold symptoms recovered almost 50 percent faster when treated by high-empathy doctors. And prostate cancer patients were discovered to have higher levels of key cancer-destroying cells (natural killer cells) in their blood three months after being seen by a doctor high in empathy, compared to patients treated by doctors lower in empathy.

So, here's the takeaway: Love, empathy, compassion, kindness – they're like superfoods for the soul. They not only make us feel better emotionally but also boost our physical health. It's like that old saying, 'Love is the best medicine.' And if it doesn't seem to work, well, increase the dose.

Sometimes, all it takes is a little kindness to make a world of difference. In a world that often undervalues these qualities, their impact is beyond measure.

Why swat a fly?

A tiny fly got stuck in my bathroom sink the other day. I hadn't seen it, and it must have been hit by a splash of water while I washed my hands. It was still alive, as it was trying to move its body, but its wings were glued to the porcelain by a film of water.

If I tried to scoop it up, its delicate wings would get torn off. So I took a piece of toilet paper and very gently dabbed away the water surrounding it. I tore off more tiny pieces of paper and dabbed the tips closer and closer to the fly, finally dabbing lightly on top of its wings to draw as much of the water off them as possible. All the while I blew very gently onto it to dry it even more.

Eventually, it seemed possible that I might be able to get it off the porcelain, so I tore off another very small piece of toilet paper, and since the area was now dry, I was able to scoop the wee fly gently off the porcelain. Its wings were still wet on the underneath, but it was alive, I thought, and I had managed not to damage its wings – as far as I could tell.

I continued to blow softly onto the paper for a few minutes to dry its wings as much as possible. But it wasn't moving. I worried that it had exhausted itself or perhaps died in panic at being stuck, unable to move, while a giant human prodded at it.

I prayed over it. I tried to mentally tell it that I was trying to help. I cupped my hands over it for a few minutes, like I was giving it healing energy and warmth from my hands. I know that may sound stupid to some, but instinct often tells you how things work.

Just when I thought my efforts had been in vain and the fly wasn't going to survive, it suddenly burst into movement. It ran rapidly across the paper. Its tiny legs moved like lightning. It did a few zigzags and then flew off the paper.

No thanks necessary.

Good vibes through good deeds

Ever had one of those days when your mood feels like it's been dunked in a vat of gray paint? One of those mornings when you forgot your coffee and felt like the walking dead? Well, there's a near-magical trick that can add a splash of color to such a dreary day, and I think you know what it might be: Yes, help someone else.

Now, I know what you're thinking: 'I'm having a rough day, and you want me to go out of my way to do something for someone else?' Stay with me here. It's not about stretching yourself thin, it's about the magic that occurs when we shift our focus.

This isn't always easy, granted. Being kind isn't always a walk in the park. Sometimes it's tough, especially when we're swamped with our own challenges or when the world seems a bit gloomy. Yet it's in these moments that kindness becomes even more vital. It's like the universe's way of saying, 'Hey, things might be tough, but here's a glimmer of hope.'

Because when you take that tiny moment to hold the door for someone, offer someone a friendly compliment, or simply share a genuine smile, something wonderful happens. Your heart feels a little lighter, and the clouds over your day begin to part.

Because sometimes, the best way to uplift yourself is by lifting others.

When you're not having the best of days

Here's something I've learned over the years: When your attention shifts onto the immediate needs of another person, it shifts away from yourself, away from your own pain, suffering, or challenges.

In that moment, you get a wee spoonful of relief, and a dose of warmth and satisfaction that comes from helping another person. It's that inbuilt Nature's reward again – the warm, fuzzy feeling you get when you help someone. It's the root of 'helper's high.'

I can recall a particularly tough day I was having. I won't go into the details, but suffice to say, my mind was swirling. I was going over and over the same stuff, having conversations with people in my mind. You know the sort of thing.

And then I saw an elderly man lying on the pavement. The sight smacked me out of myself.

I helped him to get up. He'd stumbled at the top of a flight of stairs leading up onto the pavement outside some shops. I made sure he was OK. Was he hurt? Did he need me to take him anywhere?

He assured me that he was just a wee bit shaken. He was grateful. He dusted himself off and walked into the nearby store. And that was that.

I completely forgot what I'd been worrying about moments earlier. It all seemed a bit petty now.

My problem wasn't really as much of an issue as I was making it out to be in my mind. I think a lot of our problems are like that. Sure, I'd have preferred another set of circumstances, but I'm in a much better place than a great many people who have a much tougher life, yet still manage to smile.

Helping the man who fell on the pavement lifted me out of my head. That's what kindness does when we think we're not having the best of days. It takes the focus away from our own shit onto someone else's, and sometimes it shows us a different perspective on things.

You've undoubtedly had this sort of experience yourself. And here's something else: I suspect that on more than more occasion, after this shift in perspective, you realized that it's not just that guy at work who's being an asshole, but that you've kind of been one too...

Be kind. It's almost always the right thing to do.

The gentle guide to not being an ass

In the pages of history, you won't find a single epic ballad that celebrates the perks of being an ass. But when it comes to kindness, it's been the beloved protagonist in countless tales, verses, and melodies since time immemorial.

Being an ass takes effort. All that eye-rolling, snide commenting – it's exhausting. Being nice? Easy as pie. And, as I've said before, who doesn't love pie?

Now, we've all been an ass at times. That whole 'don't judge people because you don't know what they're going through' applies to us too. Despite our best intentions, even the most determined kindness crusaders fall short when they're dealing with stuff that's overwhelming.

One day, I drove to the local post office. It's only three quarters of a mile (1.2km) away and I always walk, but that day I was short of time. There aren't many parking spaces, but by the time you've driven around a few times, someone will usually have moved.

I approached the spaces at the side of the road outside the post office. There was a large space, easily enough room for two vehicles. A car was ready to reverse into one of them. I indicated too, with the intent to let him in and then I'd pull up and reverse into the other space.

Only, he reversed into far more than one car's length, leaving no room at all for me. I still attempted to reverse in. I was trying to make a point. I had a bit of an issue with inconsiderate parking at the time that I was letting get to me. The small car park near our house only has a handful of spaces and visitors to the area frequently park in the middle of two spaces. Residents like me get frustrated.

I was also being a bit of an ass, because there was no way my car – albeit a small Mini Cooper – could possibly fit.

The other driver watched me make back and forth serpentine maneuvers for what seemed like ages, and finally, grudgingly, shifted his car a few inches forward into the five feet of space he'd left himself in front. I managed to squeeze in. Just. It was the parking equivalent of a three-point turn. Only I took about seven.

I looked into his car. I could see the top of his head over his seat. I made a slightly exasperated face and lifted my hands up. Just a little. I was torn between being kind – I do honestly try to live what I write about, but I'm also human and I don't manage so well sometimes – and expressing how I was currently feeling about some people's inconsiderate behavior.

So, I didn't make a full-on gesture. Just a sort of half-hearted shoulder shrug kind of thing. But the sort that you still regret if the person stepping out of the car turns out to be six foot six and muscled like a wrestler.

Only he wasn't six foot six. He was a frail old man who took the best part of three minutes to get himself and a walking stick out of the seat.

I felt terrible. I knew that he would have been struggling with confidence. That's why he parked in the middle of two spaces. My dad was a bit like that before he was diagnosed with the brain tumor. He'd started to lose his confidence a bit. He'd take a little more space and time than usual for maneuvers.

Suddenly, the issue I had with parking seemed petty. As I said earlier, you never know what a person is dealing with. You can never really know if someone is actually being inconsiderate. Sometimes they are. But more often they're not. Mostly, people just have a lot on their minds, and many are living through a tough couple of pages in the book of their life. Parking properly, or whatever, isn't the foremost thing on their mind right now, even if it is the central focus of yours in that instant.

You don't know either way. So cut people a bit of slack – whether it's about parking, how they lead their lives, or their dress sense. Fewer mean comments, more 'you got this, you're doing great!' shows of support.

Because here's a note of caution: I've learned that kindness usually comes back to you. It's the boomerang effect. But so too does being an ass.

Some reasons to be mindfully kind

I sometimes think of kind people like a box of chocolates from the universe. Some are sweet, some are velvety, and some come with soft centers. The taste warms the heart. And everyone loves chocolates.

But kindness is more than a sweet sensation or that healthy mug of happy hormones. Magic happens when it's let loose in our communities. Let me break it down:

1. A friendship booster

Kindness is like glue for relationships. It helps people trust, respect, and have each other's backs.

2. A community builder

Think of kindness as the magic wand that strengthens the bonds in communities and helps everyone get along. It turns neighborhoods into tight-knit communities with a 'we're in this together' vibe.

3. A peace maker

Kindness is like the superhero that smashes barriers, heals emotional wounds, and helps people from all walks of life understand each other. Whether it's a family drama or bigger societal stuff, arguments can cool down because of a few words spoken in kindness.

4. A trust builder

Kindness builds trust. We come to learn that each other's intentions are genuine and trust evolves naturally.

5. An inclusivity promoter

Kindness invites everyone to the party no matter where you're from and what you believe. It says, 'Hey, all of you are awesome!'

6. A ripple-effect creator

One act of kindness can set off a domino effect. Before you know it, everyone's doing kind things because they've caught the vibe.

All in all, a few dollops of kindness here and there can make everyone's day a wee bit brighter. In case you were wondering.

Beat the bully

All this talk about kindness is good 'n' all, but what if you're being bullied? Granted, it's a lot harder to be kind to a person who is hurting you. And I'm not necessarily recommending that course because it depends on the situation.

Sometimes, maybe. But other times – absolutely not! In some situations, the kind thing to do is be kind to yourself and get out of there, if you can, or ask for help if you can't. That's self-kindness and I'll talk a lot more about it in the next chapter, but for now, let's run with the theme of kindness to others and see where it takes us in a situation where there's bullying.

Being bullied can touch a raw nerve. I know because I've experienced it. When it comes to bullying, it's tempting to label the bully as the 'big bad wolf.' But behind the growl and sharp teeth, there's often a hurt little pup.

So instead of sharpening our claws, what if we try a different approach? Now, it's not easy just to slip on your empathy cap, because, let's face it, being picked on hurts, and the last thing you want to do in the moment is feel sorry for the plonker standing over you. But just like the latest binge-worthy series on Netflix, you don't always get the full story in the first episode. Maybe we can view bullying through a softer lens.

The power of pity

I was bullied a lot in my final year at high school. It wasn't by your classic bully. It was mostly dished out by middle-class girls and boys aged 17 and 18. It involved assaults on my mental health rather than my physical body.

Sometimes, to find solace, I took refuge in the school's lecture theatre during lunch or a free period. The theatre was only ever used for official school events, so it was empty most of the time. I went there sometimes just to be alone and cry. I'd dream that I was strong, fearless, and untouchable; that I was so powerful no one would ever dare say a wrong word to me again.

I did try to stand up for myself once or twice, but one of the bullies threatened me. He was the only one who actually *was* big and tough-looking. It happened when

I was gazing out of a large window while waiting for our chemistry teacher to let us into class at the end of the lunch hour. As I peered out of the window, my face close to the pane, the bully thumped the back of my head with the palm of his hand so hard that my face slammed into the glass. The impact almost broke my nose.

My defensive instinct was, 'Hey! What do you think you're doing?' It was met by: How dare I speak back to him! How dare I! Would I like my face smashed in? I thought he'd just done that, but I felt it best not to press the matter further.

Finding a way to endure, I turned to pity. Not self-pity, but pity for them that they felt the need to be so hurtful. It's not exactly kindness, I know, and this is supposed to be a book about kindness. But you have to start somewhere. Somewhere that gets you away from hurt and anger. It's like stepping on a ladder of emotion, where pity is one of the lowest rungs. The rungs of empathy and kindness, even happiness, are higher up, and usually out of reach when you're being treated badly.

In the darkest moments, we often cling to whatever keeps us afloat. Pity was my lifebuoy.

But here's the thing. Over the years that followed, pity evolved into empathy and compassion, like a leaf growing on an olive branch. As I matured, I realized that I couldn't have known about their lives, what it might have been like at home for some of them, or other stuff like the pressures they were under. Hurt people hurt people, after all.

I bumped into one of the bullies in a bar about ten years later. He was cold toward me. I told him that I'd struggled a lot in that year of school with the way he and his friends treated me. He said it was because I was a dick.

This is a common defense people use when they know that what they did was wrong, but they're not ready to face it. They attack you again and try to find some justification in their own mind for their behavior. Try to make you believe their actions were your own fault.

I immediately went to pity. It was never about me. They just needed someone to target as a way to deal with their own shit. And pity almost immediately grew to compassion as I stood there facing him. I smiled. Not in defiance at what he'd said, but at myself, that I'd found compassion so quickly.

I forgave them all a long time ago. I think we all at times act in ways we later come to regret. Who hasn't said or done something they wish they hadn't? We're only human, after all. And I think everyone is just trying their best in life with the knowledge and past experiences available to them, and with the pressures and constraints they're under.

Retaliation. Revenge. That's how we've become used to measuring strength. But revenge isn't strength. It's an *attempt* to feel powerful, because the reality is that we *don't* feel powerful.

True strength isn't found in seeking revenge. Hurting someone back may feel like a fleeting victory, yet the genuine, unshakable power lies in compassion – in understanding the pain of another, in rising above the hurt. It's about embracing the beauty of our shared humanity, even when faced with its darkest aspects.

Compassion is inexhaustible and it's available at any instant – if we look for it. Pity helps us find it. Once you've had a taste of that sort of power, retaliation or hurting another person is what feels weak.

Why some people think being kind means you're weak

I want to say a bit more about this, because there's this weird myth floating around in some quarters that being kind is a sign of weakness. We've gotten confused about it. In a lot of people's heads, being strong has traditionally been mixed up with being all macho and stoic.

Masculinity has come to emphasize traits like dominance, assertiveness, and emotional suppression. Some people therefore learn to think of traits such as kindness, compassion, and vulnerability as being unmanly or weak. I've known some guys to refer to kindness as a 'girly' trait and avoid showing it. I mean, 'real men' don't show emotions, do they? These guys think kindness equals crying at movies – a big no-no.

Some people even trace this 'kindness is girly and weak' belief back to Victorian times. Back then, being kind was seen as a woman's thing – think of the Victorian lady being the 'angel of the house.' Men were worried they'd lose their edge, their gravitas, if they were too nice.

You'd think this idea might come from some deep evolutionary theory, but nope! Even Charles Darwin, Mr. Evolution himself, never claimed that being kind was weak. Incidentally, the phrase 'survival of the fittest' was coined by Herbert Spencer, the English polymath, and not Charles Darwin.

What Darwin really said was that being sympathetic and working together is actually our thing as humans. He said that sympathy and cooperation are innate and crucial for our evolutionary survival. You could say, it's like teamwork made the dream work way back in the day!

Survival of the fittest has come to be misunderstood as meaning that the strongest, fastest, cleverest, most powerful, and even the most ruthless are better suited to thrive in the world – as if they have all the necessary tools. But really, survival of the fittest is about adapting and fitting in. In our modern world, this takes empathy and kindness, not physical strength.

You might argue that deep down, our biology sometimes tells us to go all 'me first!' And that might be true: On a basic biological level, displays of aggression or dominance can sometimes be protective mechanisms, rooted in our evolutionary past. Moments of fear or stress can bring out the aggressive side of human nature. But we're not in the Stone Age anymore.

We're not in the Middle Ages either. Once upon a time, kings and rulers had to play hardball. They had to make tough, unsentimental decisions 'for the greater good' – or to protect their hold on power. Being too kind might have made others think they could be easily fooled. But we're now in the 21st century.

Some people also get the wrong idea from the title of Richard Dawkins's book *The Selfish Gene*. It doesn't mean we're all out for ourselves, either. It's about how genes do their thing – they're survival machines, not conscious, reasoning people. And get this: Even though genes can be 'selfish,' they somehow made us humans – a species that leans toward being kind and caring. We're not a selfish species at all. Kindness is innate, like I said earlier.

There's another reason why people think kindness is a type of weakness. It's a version of 'hurt people hurt people.' Rather than confront their own shortcomings in the kindness arena, some people hold on to the idea that kindness is weakness because it's easier to devalue a trait, after all, than admit you're lacking in it.

All in all, some of us have developed this idea that kindness is weak and that we need more 'power tools' to get by in our world. Yet look at the example we've been set by people such as Gandhi, Rosa Parks, Martin Luther King, Malala Yousafzai, Helen Keller, and Nelson Mandela. They used compassion, kindness, and non-violence as potent tools for change.

There are times where it takes more strength to be kind, to listen, to be patient, than to react with anger or aggression. This is how we should think of strength in the 21st century.

Will I be a pushover if I'm kind?

Before we move on to the next chapter, I want to say a few more words about the idea that kindness is strength, because I feel we're on a bit of a roll with it.

Some people think that if you're kind, you're an easy target or a pushover. So let me clear the air concerning that misconception.

Kindness can be your superpower. It's that gentle nudge you give that can turn someone's day around or it's the little ray of sunshine in an otherwise cloudy sky. Having this superpower doesn't mean you let people walk all over your sparkly cape!

You see, kindness isn't just about being sweet to others; it's about standing up for what's right with grace and respect. It's in the ability to say, 'Hey, that's not cool,' with a smile and firm resolve. Kindness means understanding boundaries – yours and others'. It's a sign that you're in tune with the vibes around you, and that you choose to elevate them, rather than squash them.

Here's where it gets juicy: It's about being kind to yourself too. Oh yes! If you're always pouring love and kindness into others but forget to fill up your own cup, you'll end up running on fumes. And who wants that?

Being kind to yourself means recognizing when you need a break, saying 'no' when your plate's too full, and giving yourself a pat on the back even when things go haywire (because, hey, we all mess up sometimes!). Wear that badge of kindness with pride, but just remember to shine some of that warmth on yourself too.

Because in the grand scheme of things, a world with more kindness is a world we all want to live in. And just between us, I think the world could use a few more superheroes like you. Keep rocking that cape!

Why you should be kind to yourself

Ever heard of the 'giving a f*ck' paradox? You say you don't give a f*ck about what someone says or does, and it might be true. So you do your own thing. But on the other hand, you're prioritizing your mental health, so you are giving a f*ck – about your own mental health: That's self-kindness. On the one hand you don't give a f*ck, but on the other hand you do. It's just down to what you give your f*ck about.

I was talking about this book to a friend. She'd had a bad day.

She blurted, 'When your life feels like shit and you're struggling and something is pissing you off, kindness is the last thing on your mind. It's not easy when your own life is shit, if something painful has happened, to try to give a f*ck about someone else's life.'

She paused and then said, 'Yes, I get it, being kind is good for you and all that. La-de-f*cking-da. But right now, I don't give a f*ck.'

Then another pause, and, 'OK, how do I get to that place where I do give a f*ck? How can I get to kindness – because sometimes it's me that needs the help.'

'Maybe the answer, or at least the beginning of the answer, is to reach out,' I replied. 'Like you're doing now. It's self-kindness. I didn't know you were struggling so much.'

She didn't agree that she was reaching out, at least in the conventional way where you call a friend and ask for a chat.

'It came out in a different way, but it was still a call for help,' I said. 'You're prioritizing your mental health.'

Because even when life feels heavy and damp, reaching out can help, no matter how you do it. It's an accessible rung in the feeling-better ladder. It's being kind to yourself. It's acknowledging that you need some support. Yes, you want to get higher up the ladder, but you need to get one foot on it first. And talking to someone can help you do this.

Sometimes you can put your foot on another rung and help someone else, as I indicated in the previous chapter. But there are times when that rung is just a bit too high. There are times in life where you need to look after yourself first!

I struggled with depression once upon a time. I was working in R&D when it happened. I had always been the positive guy, the one who sees the silver lining in everything, and who cheers other people up. I was ashamed to tell anyone, so I kept it to myself.

It got so bad that I used to leave work at 4 p.m., drive home, get in my house, lock the door, draw the curtains, lie on the floor and cry. I withdrew from my friends because I struggled to maintain conversations. Depression is funny that way. And the more I worried about it, the more I'd seem to be stuck with silences. So I just stopped going out. It was one less pressure.

Mum used to phone me regularly because she had a feeling something was wrong. But I would always try to sound bouncy and say everything was great. Then, one Sunday when she phoned, I told her how I was feeling. I broke down a bit.

Mum has a lot of experience with depression. I mentioned how she'd had postnatal depression and struggled with depression for years afterward. She put on her Mum hat right then and told me to come home. So I got in my car and drove the 240 miles (390km) back. I called in sick the next morning and said I wouldn't be at work that week. Instead, I spent the days with Mum and Dad. Talking, opening up. And just lots of sitting on the sofa and watching TV. But Mum and Dad were there so it felt comforting.

And it felt good to have told someone. Relief. Like I wasn't doing it by myself anymore.

That was the beginning of my recovery. Talking to someone. It happened to be my mum and then Dad too, but mostly Mum. They had different roles. Mum's great to talk to and bounce thoughts and ideas off. Dad was good at being there, like a security blanket. I always felt safe with Dad sitting on the sofa. Comforting. Besides all this, it was the opening-up bit that mattered.

The sun didn't miraculously shine on my life the following day. I didn't feel back to normal right away. I'd forgotten what normal was, truth be told. I could barely remember not feeling heavy and dark.

It took a bit of time. Five or six months or so, if I'm being honest. I'd have a few good days and then a few bad days. Then a few more good days. Up and down, but gradually in an upward direction. And it was this experience that eventually resulted in me leaving my job altogether and becoming a writer and speaker, as I am now – a career that's much more fulfilling for me.

I learned then that sometimes when shit happens, it gives you an opportunity to reorient yourself toward the flowers. When you're deep in the shit, the smell of the flowers can be hard to find. But if you ask for help, together you might be able to pull yourself out of the crap, and you'll find your way to the flowers in the end.

Tell someone if things are shit

Talking to Mum and Dad had such a positive impact on me that I thought I'd say more about the benefits of speaking to someone when you're struggling with your mental health. It can be beneficial for a multitude of reasons. Here are a few of them:

1. Validation

Sharing your feelings and thoughts allows others to validate your experiences. It's an acknowledgment that can be crucial if you are feeling isolated or believe that no one understands what you're going through.

2. Perspective

Discussing your worries can provide a fresh perspective. Sometimes when we're mired in our problems, it can be hard to see the bigger picture or other angles. Another person, with their own perspective, might offer insights or alternative viewpoints that hadn't occurred to you.

3. Processing

The act of articulating your feelings can be therapeutic in itself. It gets stuff off your chest. Putting words to your emotions and experiences really can help clarify and process them. It helped me.

4. Structuring thoughts

Discussing your feelings and experiences out loud can also help you structure your thoughts, which can lead to better understanding and problem-solving.

5. Reduction in isolation

Mental health struggles can often make us feel isolated or alone in our experience, like when I withdrew from my friends. Talking to someone can help bridge that gap of isolation and provide a sense of connection.

6. Advice and guidance

Conversations can often lead to advice or guidance on coping strategies, resources, or potential solutions to specific problems. And you may learn that the person (or people) you speak with has also gone through some shit themselves and learned some important things about coping that they can pass on to you.

7. Release

Venting or simply 'getting things off your chest' can provide relief. Holding on to feelings or worries can be stressful, so discussing them can be like releasing a pressure valve.

8. Brain and body chemistry

Interacting with others, especially in a positive or supportive environment, can lead to the release of certain neuropeptides such as oxytocin – our kindness hormone. This helps promote feelings of bonding, safety, and connection, helps lower blood pressure, helps us digest food, speeds up healing, and a whole heap of other stuff that I mentioned earlier.

9. Responsibility sharing

Sometimes just knowing that someone else is aware of your struggles and is there to support you can make the burden feel a little lighter. It feels like you're not going through it alone.

10. Encouragement

A supportive listener can offer encouragement and hope, which can be invaluable during tough times.

11. Prevention of harm

If someone is considering self-harm or has suicidal thoughts, talking can serve as an essential intervention, guiding them toward professional help or immediate assistance.

12. Feedback loop

Conversing about your mental health can allow for feedback. Over time, as you discuss your experiences, strategies, and progress, having someone provide feedback can help you gauge your journey and make necessary adjustments. And who knows, maybe one day you'll be able to share all you've learned with someone else.

Remember too that while talking to friends and family can be beneficial, speaking with trained professionals such as therapists and counselors can provide you with specialized guidance, coping strategies, and other therapeutic techniques tailored to your individual needs.

And if you're on the other side of the fence – you're the person someone has reached out to – kindness can be as simple as being here, now, with someone who is in pain, without offering them solutions. They don't always need you to solve their problems. Nor do they want to be told to 'man up'. Some people just need to know that you're there and you're a safe shoulder to cry on.

Check in with yourself

How are you feeling today? Just thought I'd ask in case no one else has.

But really, how *are* you? We often greet others with this question but rarely direct it inwardly. Yet, amid the hustle and bustle of life, the incessant pings of our devices, and that mental to-do list that seems ever-growing, sometimes it's crucial to just... pause.

Imagine if you treated your mind like a dear friend. You wouldn't dream of going weeks without checking in on a friend, so why do it to yourself? Maybe it's time for a little mental health 'coffee break' and to make a habit of it. Picture it: A cozy chat with your own mind, maybe over an imaginary cuppa. 'Hey, Brain. How are we feeling today?'

But seriously, it doesn't have to be an elaborate ritual. You don't need a fancy meditation cushion or a yoga mat (though you can if you want) and it's OK if your idea of relaxing isn't herbal tea and wind chimes. Just the act of pausing and acknowledging how you feel is enough – a little nod to your mental well-being.

And you know what? It's completely OK if sometimes that internal conversation reveals things aren't all rainbows and unicorns. Maybe it's cloudy with a chance of meatballs. That's all right. Recognizing this is the first step, as there's power in acknowledging how we truly feel.

It's self-compassion. And it's good for your mental health. In fact, researchers from the Department of Applied Psychology and Human Development at the University of Toronto showed that practicing mindfulness together with self-compassion significantly reduced symptoms of depression. They did a randomized controlled trial that compared 78 people who practiced mindfulness and self-compassion with 87 people in a control group. Most of the participants had been diagnosed with generalized anxiety disorder and depression. After four weeks of daily practice, the ones who had practiced mindfulness and self-compassion had significantly fewer depressive symptoms compared to those who didn't practice.

The important thing with self-compassion is not to judge or chide yourself. Remember, we're treating our minds like the dear friends they are. Friends don't scold; they listen, they empathize, and sometimes they just sit in comfortable silence.

So, as you go about your day, amidst the deadlines, the chores, and, yes, even the joys, take a second. Breathe in, breathe out, and check in. Your mind deserves a little TLC and you might just walk away from that 'coffee break' feeling a tad lighter.

What is self-kindness?

I started this chapter with one form of self-kindness: speaking to someone. But there are loads of different ways we can be kind to ourselves. Life is about finding a balance, that sweet spot between being kind to others and being kind to ourselves.

Self-kindness isn't found in the same place for everyone. It depends on the context, on how you feel, where you are in your life, and any other stuff that's happening. It's about nurturing your well-being and building a positive relationship with yourself, within the context of your life. Here are a few different forms that self-kindness can take:

1. Say 'no'

Self-kindness can mean saying 'no' or walking away. It doesn't need to be a hard 'no'; it can be a 'not right now' or even a 'maybe later.' A softer 'no', but a 'no' all the same. It can also be about leaving a room, a conversation, or even a relationship.

2. Take time out

Self-kindness can be taking time for yourself, doing something that's important to you. Or just having a rest.

3. Give yourself a treat

Treating yourself in some way can be an act of self-kindness – maybe a new outfit or a pair of shoes, getting your hair done, a day trip, a spa visit, or even a warm bath, a book, and a glass of wine.

4. Social media detox

Self-kindness can be deleting a social media account, especially if it's been causing you stress. Or it can be blocking a person who is causing you stress.

5. Treat yourself with compassion

Self-kindness can be thinking of yourself in the same gentle way you think of other people when they mess up. Go easy on yourself. Everybody screws up at some point.

6. Positive self-talk

Self-kindness can be finding positive ways to talk about yourself to yourself; no more 'I'm such an idiot' and more of 'I'm doing my best,' 'I love that I'm learning,' and 'hey, I'm only human.'

7. Set healthy boundaries

Self-kindness can involve drawing a line in the sand regarding how you're willing to allocate your time or energy, or how you're willing to let people treat you. By doing this, you create a protective space that allows you to safeguard your mental and physical health, while also fostering healthier relationships with those around you.

8. Forgive yourself

As I said, everybody messes up. It's part of the human experience. So self-kindness can mean acknowledging things you've said or done, and deciding to put them behind you, just as you'd give that same advice to someone else you care about.

9. Focus on your strengths

Self-kindness can be about celebrating your strengths instead of focusing on your weaknesses.

10. Do stuff that supports your mental health

Self-kindness can lie in doing things that support your mental health. The choice to do it doubles the strength of it.

I'd like to say more about that last one, as it captures a few different ideas. I do a few things on purpose that support my mental health, such as play tennis. It's good for my physical health, but that's not the main reason

I play. I play mostly because I enjoy it and it helps me feel good about myself.

I take lessons each week from the head coach at my local tennis club, Mark Walker, and I feel that I'm improving. I can associate that improvement with choices I'm making and committed actions I'm taking, so I feel like I'm thriving. It gives me a sense of expansion and betterment that helps me to feel elevated. That's how it supports my mental health. But it's the doing it on purpose *because it supports my mental health* that makes it an act of self-kindness.

It's when you do something that you enjoy or that gives meaning for you that it becomes self-kindness. The power is in the 'on purpose' bit.

Meeting with Self

Have you ever noticed that no matter how busy you are, you always find time for people you care about? In the same way, self-kindness sometimes means finding time for yourself, no matter how busy you are.

Occasionally, when I feel I need it, I put 'Meeting with Self' in my diary. It might be a half hour, an hour – sometimes I've blocked a whole day out. I'll read a book, go for a walk, even watch a film or a few episodes of *Star Trek*.

By writing it in my diary, I'm telling my subconscious that making time for myself is important. I give this 'me time' as much importance as I would a meeting with someone else.

Why do we feel guilty about treating ourselves nicely?

OK, it's all well and good doing kind things for yourself, but some of us are busy, we have commitments, other priorities. I hear you – I know the feeling, I have the T-shirt. But as they say, you can't pour from an empty cup. We really must find a healthy balance.

So why do we feel so guilty about taking a wee bit of 'me time'? When we should be feeling great about self-care (another term for self-kindness), we end up feeling guilty. There are a few reasons that we can start to dissolve by understanding them, which frees us up to be a little kinder to ourselves. Here are some of them:

1. Old traditions

A lot of cultures say, 'Hey, think of others before yourself!' Values like selflessness, sacrifice, and service are esteemed. So, sometimes, treating yourself or taking some time to chill on the couch just feels wrong.

2. What even is self-care?

Some people don't even know where to start, while there are others who think self-care means binging on chocolates and Netflix all day (not that there's anything wrong with that). But it's more about being your best and healthiest self (mentally as well as physically), so you can be there for others too!

3. Self-care versus fancy getaways

Oh, and not all self-care is about spa trips, either. That's a common misperception. It can be, but sometimes it's just about enjoying a good book or a walk in the park.

4. We worry what others might think

And who wants to be labeled as lazy, right? But here's the thing: There's a difference between being lazy and recharging. Keep that in mind.

5. The never-ending to-do list

Let's be real: There's always something to do, isn't there? I feel this one – that I should be doing something productive rather than resting. But the fact is that if you burn out, the list is just going to get longer.

6. Being your own toughest critic

If you're always trying to be Superman or Wonder Woman, it's hard to let yourself have a moment of peace. Even superheroes need to take breaks!

7. Old habits die hard

If you grew up in a place where your needs came last or were invalidated, you might feel weird prioritizing yourself now, even if you're trying to care for your mental health.

8. The need to be needed

It feels nice to be needed. Some people derive their self-worth from being indispensable to others. Taking time for ourselves may feel like we're reducing our value or significance in others' lives. But looking after yourself means you have more in the tank for helping others.

9. Job worries

In some work cultures, especially where job security is a concern, taking time off (even if deserved) can be seen as a luxury or a sign of not being fully committed to the job. Yet we all need a breather now and then.

10. Misguided altruism

Lastly, there's this idea that the more you give, the better person you are; that there's virtue in continuously giving or sacrificing without replenishing yourself. But if you're running on empty, how much can you really give?

I say all this so that next time you feel guilty about having a bubble bath or a short nap, remember – it's not just OK, it's necessary! It's crucial to internalize the idea that self-care isn't selfish; it's a necessary component of a balanced life.

No rain, no flowers

Self-kindness is also about recognizing that not being happy every day doesn't mean you've failed in life. I say this because there's a pressure in society today that nudges us into believing that if we're not constantly beaming with happiness, we're somehow failing at life; that success equals happiness. But let me tell you a little secret: That's a load of crap.

Think of a time when you stood outside right after it'd poured with rain: There's this indescribable freshness in the air, everything looks cleaner, brighter, and then, if you're lucky, you might even catch a glimpse of a rainbow. None of those magical moments would be possible without the rain. No rain, no rainbows. No rain, no flowers!

Life's no different. Those cloudy days, the emotional thunderstorms, the moments when you feel a bit waterlogged – they're all a part of your growth. Downpours of emotion and challenge often lead to the most radiant moments of clarity, understanding, and blooming. Heck, some of our best lessons come from the most torrential life downpours.

Do you need to be happy 24/7 to lead a successful, meaningful life? Absolutely not. Happiness is just one emotion in the vast palette that paints the intricate portrait of your life. It's OK to feel down, confused, or unsure. It's normal. It's OK to have days where you need an umbrella, or maybe even a boat.

Remember, just as flowers need both sunshine and rain to grow, we need a mix of experiences to truly blossom. Next time you're feeling a bit under the weather, say to yourself: This too shall pass, and after the rain, flowers will bloom. Stay vibrant, and always keep your chin up!

There's also a particular handy skill in life that's about being OK with whatever is happening. It's not everyone's cup of tea; I know I'm not OK with *everything* that happens. But if we can be OK with a lot of what happens – to be accepting of stuff, to accept people as they are – it helps. It's a sort of magic wand, because once you get good at it, a whole load of stress, irritation, annoyance, and frustration just falls away.

Now, some of this depends on what else is going on in your life. But that closed road which means you're going to be 15 minutes late for an appointment? The lack of response to that important email you sent yesterday? The smear of tomato sauce on the kitchen table? Not the end of the world. It's worth at least trying to be OK with a lot more things. It's about getting better at being OK with stuff that you're usually not OK with it, everyday stuff that makes you feel pissed or frustrated. It's a bit of mental self-care, when you let yourself chill a wee bit.

You can still strive for the things you want, but with this as your background mantra: 'I'm OK with whatever happens today.' You might not believe it right now, but when you use it in your life, you'll come to realize it's quite a handy mindset to cultivate. It's not the only happiness formula on life's blackboard, but it works a lot of the time: *It's pissing with rain and I'm going to get soaked; I'm OK with what's happening.* Or, *I've just been given a raise at work – awesome; I'm OK with what's happening.* Be OK with the good and with the shit.

It's just a little mindset that helps you to be less resistant to what's happening. It doesn't mean you can't celebrate the good. But rejoice, have a few beers, and then come back to yourself.

Ups and downs are normal. They're written into the human experience, deep in the human psyche. We expect a push and pull. Like the ocean tides, the in and out of the breath, the beat of the heart, night and day, everything has cycles. We evolved within cycles of in and out, up and down. We've come to expect them in every aspect of life. It's why shit sometimes lands before success.

So don't be afraid of the shit. It's normal. Welcome it. Because it too will pass, to make way for the next wave of good stuff.

Don't be upset if it's raining in your life. The sun will shine again. That's what the sun does. No rain, no flowers!

I was thinking of my dad when I started writing this section. Him having a brain tumor and eventually passing away was shit. It was shit for Mum especially, because she'd never been alone. But time heals. And the sun comes out again.

About a month before he passed away, I sat with him one night so Mum could have a break and go to the bingo with her friends. I asked him about his younger days. He told me about playing football.

His team, Holy Cross, Croy, won the John Thomson Memorial Trophy in 1962. It was the equivalent of the Scottish Cup for the tier he played in. Dad scored in the final and several times on the way there. He was lucid when he talked about it that night and proud of his achievement, even though the tumor played with his mind a bit.

He went upstairs and came down with the cup. He gave it to me and said it was mine now. I recognized it instantly. My older sister, Lesley, and I played with it when we were children. It was missing the base because we broke it. Neither of us admitted to it at the time. I think it was my sister who broke it, but it might have been me. Water under the bridge now.

I treasure that cup. And the fact it's broken. That's family life. It makes it even more special.

Things have picked up. It's a year on. We've got more used to Dad not being here. And I have the John Thomson Memorial Trophy on my desk.

No rain, no flowers.

Accept yourself

I wrote a book a few years ago called *I Heart Me: The Science of Self-Love*. Unbeknownst to my publisher and the people who read my books, I was struggling with my own self-love or self-esteem. (I use self-love interchangeably with self-esteem: that inner sense of your own worthiness and value.) Writing it was cathartic and healing. It changed me on many levels.

One of my realizations was there's nothing wrong with you if you have problems and challenges in life that you struggle to get through. It means you're human. Shit happens to everyone. But many of us overthink and believe nearly everyone else is living it up.

We make too many comparisons with other people: 'If only I was like Joe and could earn money so easily.' 'If only our house was as big as Claire's.' 'If only I could eat the way Amy does and not put on weight.' 'If only my life was as easy as Pete's.'

But there's one golden nugget that I want to share here. Imagine for a moment that life is this massive cosmic theatre and we're all given roles to play. Now, what happens if you're busy trying to pinch Jane's costume or Emma's accent – chaos, right? Not only do you mess up your lines, but you also rob everyone else of the unique character you're meant to play.

It's a bit like trying to force a cactus to bloom like a rose. First off, ouch. Secondly, without our prickly pal doing its thing, we've nowhere to get those desert vibes.

Oscar Wilde, that legendary wit, once said, 'Be yourself; everyone else is already taken.' I reckon he was onto something. There's no point spending your days chasing after the reflection of someone else when you've got your own shimmering essence. It's like wanting to be the moon when you shine just as brilliantly as a star.

Don't think you're a shining star? Sure, we all have our doubts and shadows – those sneaky thoughts whispering, 'You're not enough,' or, 'You should be more like so-and-so.' But if everyone took that advice, we'd be living in a world of clones and, frankly, that sounds like a sci-fi movie gone wrong.

Life's too short, and you're too cool to wear someone else's shoes, especially if they're a size too small. Embrace your quirks, celebrate your edges, and remember: The world needs your flavor. So sprinkle it everywhere and make life a bit zestier! Stay awesome and, most importantly, stay You!

Who cares if someone doesn't like you?

While we're on the general theme, let's talk about another pretty important concept: Not everyone has to like you. I know, I know. That sounds a tad rebellious, but hear me out.

Imagine trying on a pair of shoes that everyone's raving about – only to find they don't fit quite right. Your toes squish, your heel slips, and every step feels like a miniature torture. The world's favorite shoes just aren't your thing. That's how trying to be everyone's cup of tea can feel too: uncomfortable, unnatural, and a teensy bit painful.

Now, think of slipping into your favorite pair of trainers. The ones that have seen better days but fit you like a dream. That's the feeling of being unapologetically you. No pretenses, no filters, just pure, genuine You-ness. It's comfy, right?

The truth is, life isn't a popularity contest (even though sometimes it feels like high school never really ended). When we go around trying to get everyone to like us, we often end up muting the quirks and qualities that make us, well, us.

Here's the reality: Some people will like you, some will adore you, some won't, and that's totally OK. If someone doesn't like you for who you are, it's usually more about their perspective than your worth. Prioritize those relationships that uplift and support you.

By being yourself, you'll naturally gravitate toward the people who appreciate and love the real you. These people are your tribe. They get your jokes, embrace your quirks, and wouldn't have you any other way. And that kind of magic is worth way more than a hundred lukewarm interactions any day.

You do You. Let your unique flag fly high. Because then the people meant for you will see your flag, love it, and come running toward it with their own equally unique flags flapping in the wind. And together, you'll make quite the colorful parade.

Self-kindness can be fierce

Before we go any further in the book, I want to say one really important thing that will help us going forward. It's about how when we talk about kindness in society, there's often this image of softness, gentleness, maybe even a touch of fragility – like picturing someone tending to a delicate flower or whispering sweet affirmations to a baby bird. But here's the twist: Self-kindness can also be downright fierce.

Let me break it down. Maybe you've had one of those days where you're your own harshest critic; you spilled your coffee, sent an email with a typo that totally changes its meaning, or missed a deadline. And instead of offering yourself a little grace, you dove deep into the 'why-can't-I-get-it-right' rabbit hole.

Now imagine if during that inner turmoil, your self-kindness roared in like a lion, drowning out those doubts with a thunderous, 'Enough! You're only human and doing your best!' That's fierce self-kindness.

Think about the times you've pushed yourself too hard, maybe burning the midnight oil for weeks on end or skipping meals just to cross off one more task. What if self-kindness wasn't just a gentle, 'It's OK, take a break,' but a passionate shout of, 'Stop! You deserve rest and care!' Or a loud, rapturous, 'No more!' A line carved into the stone with a pneumatic drill of positive determination.

Being fiercely kind to yourself is like being that protective older sibling who won't let anyone – especially your own inner critic – mess with their little brother or sister. It's about standing up against societal pressures that insist you must always be more, do more, and hustle harder. It's saying, 'I value myself too much to let anything or anyone, including my own doubts, drag me down.'

Next time you think of self-kindness, don't just picture the gentle caress of a soothing hand. Envision a roaring flame, a powerful wave, a force of Nature that fiercely asserts, 'I am enough, I do enough, and I deserve kindness, especially from myself.' Remember: Soft or fierce, self-kindness is a strength. Embrace it, amplify it, and let it roar!

The sweet spot

There's a balance – a sweet spot – between being kind to others and being kind to yourself. Sometimes it doesn't seem to matter, but sometimes it does. It's a bit like discovering the perfect recipe for a delicious dessert. You know, the kind that's just the right amount of sweet without being overwhelming. Well, life is a bit like that too.

Let's keep running with the dessert analogy. Imagine you're baking a cake. Being kind to others is like adding all those wonderful ingredients that make the cake taste amazing – the flour, the sugar, the eggs, and that dash of vanilla for extra flavor. It's about being there for your friends, lending a helping hand, and spreading positivity wherever you go. Just like the cake batter, kindness to others is the foundation of a delightful life.

But you can't forget about yourself in the mix. Being kind to yourself is like giving the cake a chance to bake properly. You need to treat yourself with care, listen to your needs, adjust the temperature, and practice self-compassion. It's the equivalent of checking the cake's progress in the oven, making sure it's not overdone or undercooked. Because if you neglect yourself, you might end up feeling burned out or underappreciated.

In the grand recipe of life, we need to remember to sprinkle kindness generously, not only outward, but inward too. And find that sweet spot where your heart feels light, your soul feels nourished, and your actions create ripples of goodness in the world. Because in the end, a life well balanced is a life well lived, just like a perfectly baked cake is a joy to savor.

The gentle power of 'no'

I mentioned earlier how self-kindness can sometimes be about saying 'no.' Picture this: It's a cozy evening, your favorite pajamas are calling your name, and you've got that brand-new book you're itching to dive into. Then *buzz*, a message pops up: 'Hey! Fancy coming out tonight?'

We've all been there – that delicate seesaw between wanting to please others and wanting to honor our own needs. Sometimes, we might feel a pressure to say 'yes,' because isn't that what good friends do?

But let's talk about the underrated power of saying 'no.' And not just any 'no,' but the gentle, soft 'no' that's draped in kindness – both for yourself and the person on the other end.

I think we can agree by now that self-kindness isn't just about bubble baths and chocolates (though those can be awesome, too). It's about recognizing our boundaries, our needs, and our limits. It's about ensuring that our cup remains full so we can keep pouring into others'.

Now, don't get me wrong. This isn't a campaign against saying 'yes' or embracing spontaneity. It's more about realizing that it's OK to choose ourselves first, even if that means declining an invite or asking for some time. So, the next time you're faced with a similar decision, remember that a 'no' doesn't have to be delivered with the force of a sledgehammer. It can be as soft as a feather, a gentle reminder that you're looking out for your well-being.

After all, a soft 'no' is still a form of self-kindness. And that's important. It's OK to prioritize yourself. The next time you say 'no,' just do it with a sprinkle of kindness. It might just be the sweetest thing you do for yourself all day.

Is self-sacrifice always a kind act?

Let's keep going with the whole sweet-spot thing. Suppose you're seated in your favorite chair with a warm mug in hand, flipping through a novel. In between the action-packed scenes and tear-jerking moments, you come across tales of heroes and heroines sacrificing everything for the greater good. It's inspiring – the noble idea of putting others before ourselves – but here's a little food for thought: Is self-sacrifice *always* a kind act?

The instinct to help, to uplift, and to protect is one of the most beautiful aspects of human nature. And self-sacrifice can often be a true act of love and kindness. But let's consider the flip side.

Imagine a candle. When it burns, it provides light and warmth to its surroundings. If it burns too fast, it exhausts itself prematurely, leaving the room in darkness. And that's a bummer for the people still eating their meal. Similarly, if we constantly neglect our needs and well-being, we might find that we have little light left to give.

Overextending ourselves can lead to burnout, resentment, and a diminishing capacity to offer genuine care. At times, our obsession with appearing selfless can stem from seeking validation or avoiding confronting our own needs. But when self-sacrifice becomes a compulsive behavior rather than a conscious choice, that's when we may need to pause and reflect.

Furthermore, constant self-sacrifice can inadvertently send the message to loved ones that their well-being matters more than ours. This might saddle them with guilt or teach them that neglecting oneself is the norm.

So, while self-sacrifice can indeed be a beautiful and kind act, it's essential to strike a balance. To truly care for others, we must also care for ourselves. The next time you think about going the extra mile for someone else, ask yourself: 'Am I running on empty?' If the answer is yes, maybe it's time to refill your cup before pouring for others. Cheers!

Kindness is infinite... but your energy isn't!

It's no secret by now that I think kindness is a universal quality and as vast as the universe itself. The universe has no boundaries, and neither does the kindness within us. But the twist is that while kindness may know no end, your personal energy is more like your phone battery. Even if you've got the latest and greatest model, it's bound to need recharging eventually.

Don't get me wrong – showering the world with your goodwill is fantastic. I'm right there with you, cheering on Team Kindness! I'm all for holding doors, giving compliments, and sending those uplifting texts at 2 a.m. to reassure a friend. But even superheroes need to recharge sometimes (I'm looking at you, Peter Parker). And it's crucial to remember this balance.

For starters, continuously giving without replenishing your reserves might leave you drained, burned out, or even resentful. Think of it like pouring water from a pitcher. If you don't occasionally refill it, soon you'll be shaking the last few drops out, wondering where it all went.

Plus, when you're running on empty, the quality of your kindness might unintentionally take a nosedive. Instead of wholehearted love, you might offer a half-hearted smile. Instead of listening with both ears, maybe you're just offering one. Or worse, you're only half-listening while you're mentally grocery shopping for tomorrow's dinner.

The solution is to remember to be kind to yourself too. Take a walk, read a book, have a coffee break, meditate, or even just nap. Refill your energy cup however you see fit. And remember, there's no shame in setting boundaries. It's not selfish; it's self-care.

In the end, by preserving and revitalizing your energy, you're ensuring that the kindness you spread is genuine, profound, and ever-flowing. Because while kindness is indeed infinite, it's best served fresh from a well-rested heart.

Don't let other people's behavior change you

Imagine it's a sunny day and you've got a delicious ice cream cone in your hand. You're about to take that exquisite first bite, and suddenly – plop! – a bird overhead decides your ice cream is the perfect spot to, you know, do its business (as nearly happened to my face this morning, when I was out walking my dog). You could think, 'That's it! Birds are the worst! I'm going to eat my meals indoors forever!' But that would mean letting one naughty bird dictate your sunny-day joys.

It's a bit like when someone dishes out a dose of unkindness. Sure, it can feel like a cloud just appeared over you. But if we let every unkind word or deed change our very essence, we're handing over our metaphorical remote control to whoever upset us. And do we really want Bossy Bertie, Negative Nellie, or Selfish Susie to have that kind of power?

I get it, it's easier said than done. It's not about being a doormat; standing up for yourself can be gold, an act of self-kindness. But transforming into an unkind person in return – that's like letting the pooping bird win. So, if someone tries to rain on your parade, remember your ice cream. Enjoy your sun, guard your cone, and maybe carry a little napkin (or a lot of grace) for the unforeseen messes. Stay sweet! Because you're way too cool to let the birds – or the occasional grump – spoil your fun.

'Humble' doesn't mean 'small'

Humility is an endearing quality, which is why many of us want to embrace it. The trouble is that we get our thinking about it tangled up. Being humble doesn't mean you need to be small, whatever you've been told. A friend told me that when she was growing up, she'd been told to be small – that it was virtuous. (It's funny how we carry simple ideas we pick up in childhood right through to adulthood. Ideas stick: I was in my thirties before I realized that an apple tree wouldn't actually grow inside me if I ate apple seeds.)

Think about it. You can excel at what you do and still be humble, and kind, and chilled. Yet a lot of us get our thinking tangled up with 'the meek shall inherit the Earth' and all that; we believe we have to downplay ourselves to be humble. But nope, that's not it.

Being humble is like, 'Yeah, I'm good at this, but I also have things to learn.' It's not about putting yourself down or acting like you're less. It's being real and genuine. It's a strength move, honestly. When you're acting small, it's more like, 'I'm not good enough,' which isn't the same vibe. Humility is good. Downplaying yourself? Not so much.

There's a quote from Buddha that goes something like, 'One genuine word is way cooler than a thousand fake ones.' All right, I'm paraphrasing. I can't remember his exact words, but it's all about keeping it real versus showing off. So, be kind to yourself. Embrace humility, but don't shrink back. It's about that sweet spot again. Celebrate your successes; just don't be an asshole.

It's the little things

Before we move on to the next chapter, here's some general life advice to help you feel better. It's about how, when we zoom out and look at life, it's easy to get caught up in the big stuff – major milestones, huge decisions, the big 'aha!' moments. But that's not really what's important.

I've been thinking about this while working on this book and found myself reflecting on the day my first book was published. While the actual event of the publication itself was exciting, there were millions of important moments before it: writing for months in the middle of the night (for a while it was the only time I could find) with my laptop, a candle, and some strong coffee; how my partner and my family supported me writing it; the feedback I received from friends on my early drafts; the days spent editing, the highs and lows, the rejections from publishers; writing in coffee shops, writing in the park when it was sunny, and much more.

It's so easy to focus on the seemingly big stuff in life, but it's the little things that matter most. These are what we actually end up reflecting back on or regretting that we missed.

Take, for instance, the small gestures we experience every day: a friend giving you a gentle pat on the back; the smile you share with someone in passing; when someone says they like your hair or your jacket; or a call from a family member just to say hello. On their own, they might not seem like much, but when we pile them all up, these are the things that warm our hearts and make our memories.

The tiniest things can make our day, like the smell of coffee brewing when we wake up (well, it does it for me at least), birds putting on a morning concert, the feel and smell of your favorite old book, or a dog licking your face to tell you it's time to get out of bed.

A moment ago, as I wrote that last sentence, my dog, Daisy, made a little whine, which is her way of saying, 'Daddy, rub my tummy.' So I did. Maybe she sensed I was thinking about her. It's these details that add a touch of color and joy to our daily grind.

I find that by really tuning in to these small moments, I start to see the world a bit differently. I feel more gratitude for my life and for the people who I share it with. It's like suddenly seeing the world in fine HD, instead of the grainy standard definition when we're only looking at the bigger things. Paying attention to all the little wonders that we usually zoom past makes life richer and more fun.

So, while the big moments have their spotlight and are important, let's not forget that it's those day-to-day tidbits that make life genuinely beautiful. They remind us that we're all in this together, and that there's beauty in the seemingly ordinary.

Let's cherish the little things more, shall we?

Lead with kindness

My dad worked in the building trade for about 50 years. He worked full time right up until he retired, when he was 70 years old.

He helped my partner and me renovate an old cottage a few years later. It was the first property we had ever owned. Dad and I worked side by side for months. It's one of my fondest memories of him. I felt like his apprentice, because my entire DIY experience prior to that had amounted to wiring a plug (clumsily) and changing a couple of lightbulbs. It was one of the most rewarding experiences of my life, as I got to be with Dad every day and learn building and joinery skills that I'll have forever.

There was one day when he told me a story of something that had happened to him at work just a few years before he retired. Dad had worked for most of his life as a concrete finisher, and one of the jobs he did was to lay and level the floors of shopping malls and stores. Once, while the company was building a new store, an underground water pipe ruptured. People started panicking because the water would soon spill out onto the road and disrupt town center traffic. That would be a disaster.

Dad heard the commotion. With some quick thinking, he climbed down into the hole and used a crowbar to push against the pipe and partially stem the flow. But water was still spewing out, albeit a little less furiously.

He had a batch of concrete already made up for the new floor. Rather than use it for its intended purpose, he diverted some of it on top of the ruptured pipe. The concrete was thick and it quickly sealed the rupture. The spewing stopped. Everyone was relieved. Job done! Afterward, Dad went back to work, dripping wet, and finished his shift.

The following day, the CEO of the company turned up at the site. He introduced himself and shook Dad's hand. He'd come all the way from head office, about 30 miles (50km) away, to see Dad and to thank him personally. Dad's actions had saved the company a lot of bother.

Dad shrugged it off. 'It was nothing,' he said. But the CEO assured him that it was a very big deal. It had taken courage and quick thinking. He was genuinely grateful. He asked if he could have his photo taken with Dad and if the photo could go in the company newsletter.

They spent some time chatting after that. The CEO asked Dad about his job, what he did and how long he had been with the company. He asked him about his family too. Dad told him that my mum and three sisters had all worked for the NHS, and then said, 'My son is a doctor.' (As I said earlier, he would always say that.)

Dad had been a blue-collar worker all his life. He told me that this was the first time he didn't feel like 'just a worker.' While it wasn't ever explicitly stated, there was a division between blue-collar and white-collar workers in every company Dad had worked with. It was implied, from the way they had always been spoken to, that blue-collar workers were somehow less than white-collar workers – less important, less valuable. More expendable. If you made a mistake, you got told off. If you missed a few shifts for any reason, you got laid off. Simple as that. To Dad, with me being so highly qualified, a Ph.D., a scientist, and now a writer of books, I think I represented us – our family – being at the top in some way. Maybe that's why he took such pride in telling people I was a doctor.

Dad felt important that day when the CEO came to see him. Respected. Appreciated. Valued. It really mattered to him. What made such an impression on him was the fact that the 'top man,' as Dad called him, came to see him *in person* to say thanks.

Dad was a quiet and humble man. In the ten years or so that had gone by since the burst pipe, he had barely told anyone about it. He only mentioned it to me now in passing, not to big up what he did, but to emphasize the kindness of the CEO in coming to visit him. It didn't cost anything for the CEO to come and say thanks to Dad, yet the impact of his kindness went a long way. His actions capture what I think of as leading with kindness. I reckon we could all do well to lead like that.

Imagine if we helped each other to feel valued and respected, to feel that what we do matters; to help each other feel included and part of it all; to trust people and let them learn. We could start just by remembering to say thank you; by being respectful of people's needs, beliefs, and feelings. By listening to them and encouraging them. This is how we will start to create a culture of kindness – whether at home, at work, in our communities, in the world – and bring out the best in each other.

Lift others when you can. You never know how much it will mean to them. Kindness doesn't need to cost anything. A seemingly small act or a few simple encouraging words may seem small to you, but they can be huge for the other person – exactly what that person needs that day.

In a culture that feels safe, friends and colleagues will stretch themselves, and tap into their creativity and inner resources in ways unavailable to them in more restricted or fearful cultures. In any business and organization, it's a route to creative and unexpected solutions.

What's more, you don't need to wait for someone at the top to declare that we should all start being kinder. Start wherever you are. Kindness is highly contagious. Small actions can quickly spread to generate large changes.

Leading with kindness: It's easier than you think!

One day, after giving a talk about kindness and mental health at a company event, I had a chat with one of the senior managers. I had just shared the above story about my dad, and the guy said he really wanted to be a kind leader. The thing was, he wasn't really sure what it meant.

'Shouldn't I already know this stuff?' he asked me. He explained he felt a bit stupid about asking his colleagues – nobody wants to seem clueless in front of their team. Yet he came across as so warm and genuine that I reckoned he already was a kind leader without knowing it.

'It's basically about how you treat people,' I told him. 'If you're nice to people while you do your job, you're leading with kindness.'

I think a lot of people who are in leadership roles already lead with kindness without even realizing it (whereas there are some who might need a tiny nudge in the right direction). Being kind applies to life in general. It's only the context that changes. The rules are the same.

The guidelines in this chapter apply just as much to how you interact with loved ones, friends, and family as they do if you work in a business or organization.

Let's start with an analogy. Say you're at the helm of a ship (or if ships aren't your thing, maybe a starship like the *Enterprise*). As the captain, you've got a choice. You can be the gruff, shouty type, barking orders left and right. Or you can be the kind, approachable captain who listens, supports, shows respect, and inspires. Which crew do you think is going to work (or in space terms, blast) harder for you? Exactly. The latter.

As we already know, leading with kindness doesn't mean you're a big softie or a pushover. Sometimes, leadership requires having to make tough decisions. Sometimes you need to ask things of people that they might not really want to be do, nor agree with. But if you communicate with empathy, listen, be honest, treat people with respect, and ask them to work with you, that's being kind.

Here are a few tips for leading with kindness:

1. Listen actively

Kindness starts with lending an ear. And not just an 'uh huh' while you scroll through your phone or read emails. I mean *really* listen. Understand the underlying message, empathize, and respond.

2. Say thank you

Saying thank you seems basic, but you'd be amazed how many people forget this. A simple 'thank you' can be gold. It can help someone feel that what they do matters. We all need to hear this from time to time. 'Thank you' can turn someone's day around.

3. Be constructive, not destructive

Feedback's important, but there's a world of difference between 'This doesn't work' and 'I love where you're going with this! Maybe we can tweak this part a bit?'

4. Open door, open heart

An open-door policy is great, but having an open heart is crucial too. Make your team or the people who rely on you feel that they can come to you with anything, anytime. My Ph.D. professor back in the day took this approach and it made the world of difference. It encouraged creativity and as a result our lab made some cool scientific breakthroughs.

5. Small gestures, big impact

Remember birthdays. Check in if someone's feeling under the weather. Celebrate achievements, no matter how small. These gestures matter.

6. Be genuine

People can spot fake kindness from a mile away. If you're going to be kind, mean it. Remember Nature's catch-22!

7. Encourage growth

This means creating opportunities, understanding mistakes as learning curves, and providing resources for your team to flourish.

8. Kindness is contagious

By leading with kindness, you also set a tone that ripples through the team, department, or company. Before you know it, your entire crew (or spaceship) will be spreading kindness like confetti!

9. Be vulnerable

Lastly, you don't always need to act like you have all the answers. Say when you don't. Heck, even admit that you're trying to be a kind leader and ask if your team could be patient with you. Being honest and vulnerable disarms people. Rather than take advantage, most people will want to work with you even more, because it gives them permission to be themselves too.

One more thing: Kindness isn't just a leadership style, it's a way of life. As the captain of your ship, set sail for a world where kindness isn't just an act, but a habit. Safe sailing! (Or blasting through the cosmos!)

Some ways that businesses can be kind

You might be wondering if it's possible to blend kindness into the core of a business, institution, household, or community.... Remember, kindness is kindness and only the context changes. Kindness is good for everyone's health, it fosters a positive environment, and it can also improve customer satisfaction (as the people you interact with will enjoy interacting with you), employee retention (people in your team, circle, community, will want to stick around), and overall organizational success. Go kindness!

But how do we introduce kindness into a business or other organization on a practical level? Some of the suggestions that follow might fit perfectly where you work. Some might not. Some might even inspire a few more creative ideas. But as we know, one-size-fits-all policies don't always work. Each leader, team, department, or group will have different constraints and contexts to work within. A general decision to work with kindness is the right thing, but how that looks for each team, department, or section of a company or community might be different.

First off, leaders have to lead. You've likely heard the phrase 'lead by example' – leadership sets the tone. If the bosses are rocking the kind approach, everyone else will want to join the party.

Encourage some kindness initiatives. Create a committee or task force, like your own kindness squad, who'll be on the lookout for ways to inject some kindness and good vibes into the workplace or club. Maybe host some fun workshops! Think of them as kindness boot camps. Dive deep into stuff like empathy, good old communication skills, and how not to lose your cool.

And recognize kindness where it already exists. Implement a system that acknowledges employees and others who go above and beyond in showing kindness to others, whether that's through peer nominations or customer feedback.

Be kind to your team. Maybe introduce flexible work hours. Let's face it, we all sometimes need a day in our pajamas. It can be therapeutic to work from your couch sometimes. Why not go all out and offer mental health days? Colleagues could get an allocation of paid time to do whatever they want that they feel will support their health. And maybe even offer some kind of a 'we've got your back' system that provides counseling and resources for employees going through personal struggles. Because, let's be honest, life's a roller coaster and even when a team member shows up every day, they might be working through a tough chapter in their life. So let your team know: 'We're in this together.'

While at work, encourage regular breaks and provide somewhere employees can go to relax. A chill-out zone would be epic. Comfy bean bags and calming tunes won't be every company's cup of tea, but could be just the tonic if it's practical.

Try out mindfulness Monday, kindfulness Friday (there's no weekday beginning with a 'k', but Fridays are cool. Go Fridays!), or even yoga Tuesday. These practices can help individuals respond in kinder ways in stressful situations.

Employees might want to feel that their job does some good in the community. So team up for a community day. Clean a park, paint a school. It's like a team-building retreat but with more heart. Engaging with the community fosters a sense of purpose and spreads kindness beyond the confines of the business.

Let's not forget diversity and inclusion. Emphasize the importance of understanding and respecting differences. Everyone's unique, so make everyone feel welcome. The more, the merrier!

You could offer mentoring where newbies are paired up with veterans to support them in the early days. This will help create a sense of belonging and ease the transition into the company culture, like a big bro, big sis, sort of thing, or like high school buddies but minus the awkward teenage phase.

When it comes to the bigger stuff, ensure that changes – especially those that directly affect employees (or other group members) – are communicated transparently. This shows respect and builds trust. It's a bit like being treated to a glass-bottom boat trip, but for company news.

Finally, when was the last time you looked at the rule book? Rules with heart rock. Maybe it's time for a sprinkle of kindness there, too. Review company policies and ensure they reflect values of kindness and empathy. For instance, you could have policies that support employees during personal hardships.

Also, remember that kindness in business isn't about letting everyone walk all over you. It's about facing challenges with a big heart, keeping it real, and knowing that good vibes bring good business. It means approaching challenges with empathy, maintaining integrity, and prioritizing relationships. In the end, a business built on kindness can create lasting value for its stakeholders, its community, and the world at large.

The world's a much brighter place with a dash of kindness. So let's make it shine at work.

Can you win in business while being kind?

It's been said that nice guys finish last. The assumption is that people who are kind and gentle will get outmaneuvered by the cutthroat businessman. I suppose the belief here is that you need to be ruthless and aggressive to win. But I don't think that's true at all.

Imagine for a moment the sort of colleague you'd love to work with – would it be someone who cuts corners, talks behind your back, and steps on others to get ahead? Or would it be someone who's always there with a kind word, a helping hand, and a collaborative spirit? Chances are, most of us would choose the latter. And if your own stamp increases and your influence rises, who are you going to recommend for a higher position?

Being kind doesn't mean you're weak. It means listening actively, fostering collaboration, and building relationships. I don't see much weakness there! What I see is intelligence and strength. Kindness can pave the way for more robust networks, stronger team dynamics, and a positive organizational or community culture.

Heck, even your local Zumba club, five-a-side football, trivia quiz, or bingo nights are more enjoyable when kind people are around. I play in a local tennis league; everyone wants to win, but we play with fairness and joke around with heart.

Look at some of the most successful businesses today. Behind their mega corporations and innovative products, many are built on values of empathy, collaboration, and community engagement. Kindness is finding its way into the heart of more and more businesses as a visible company value.

When the pandemic first hit, all my public speaking events were canceled. It was a financial blow and I worried about how to keep afloat. Then the theme of Mental Health Awareness Week in the UK was announced as 'kindness.' All of a sudden, I was inundated with requests to give online talks for companies during that week and afterward, all on the subject of kindness. I was surprised at just how many companies were interested in learning about kindness, its health benefits, and how it would work in their environments.

Many of us only see the front end of a company, like looking in a shop window where we don't get to know the personalities who decorated it. But today many organizations, clubs, and communities are actively working behind the scenes to build cultures of kindness. Nowadays, the modern consumer isn't just buying a product; they're buying into a brand's ethos, its story, and its integrity. That's what we're looking for. In a world where kindness is moving further toward center stage, we're looking to do business with any group or organization who flies with a badge of kindness on its lapel.

Moreover, employees today seek more than just a paycheck. They want to work for companies that care not just about their bottom line but about their people and the wider community. A kind business attracts talent, fosters loyalty, and boosts morale.

Kindness also fosters innovation. When people feel safe, valued, and respected, they'll share ideas, take risks, and think outside the box. A cutthroat environment, on the other hand, often leads to fear, reduced creativity, and stagnation.

Of course, being kind doesn't mean letting others walk all over you, as I said earlier. It can require setting boundaries, communicating clearly, and leading with compassion. It means understanding that everyone, including yourself, has room to grow, and that growth is best achieved in a nurturing environment.

So, next time you hear that 'nice guys finish last,' take a moment to rethink. In the world of business, where relationships are currency and collaboration is king, kindness might just be the ace up your sleeve. In the end, the race isn't always to the swift or the battle to the strong, but to those who know the power of genuine human connection.

Here's to the nice guys and gals, because maybe, just maybe, they've been winning all along.

Kindness in politics

OK, so we're doing kindness in business. Let's go all out: What about kindness in politics? Can there ever be such a thing?

Well, first off, politics isn't just about policies and votes; nor does it only involve political leaders and political parties. We all have to navigate politics, whether it be family or office politics, so the same principles of kindness apply. Only the context changes.

A lot of real life involves bargaining, making concessions, voicing our opinions, and supporting other people's positions. At the end of the day, politics at any level is about people. And people remember kindness. So, if you ever find yourself in a political storm, try to be the lighthouse of kindness, and watch how this lights up and transforms the atmosphere and landscape around you. Because even in the most challenging arenas, a touch of kindness can make a world of difference.

Hit the right note

One last thing before we head on over to the next chapter: Let's talk about emails and their tone. How often does the tone of an email get lost and a positive intention come across as blunt? Especially when the person doesn't mean it that way. Maybe you're short on time and your one-line reply is misconstrued, or your paragraph to Mike asking if he can set up a meeting with Donna comes across as a demand. You don't have the advantage of that disarming smile or those kind eyes that you get in real life. When we're face to face, or even on the phone or a video call, it's easy to know the difference. But with words on a screen, any sentence can be up for debate. They can leave the receiver wondering if they are liked or valued.

But maybe you *can* put that kind smile in an email to soften the tone. Perhaps you think a smiley emoji isn't very professional. Says who? Add it anyway and you might start a trend. The boss is human too and maybe she has kids with colorful toys lying all around her living-room floor. A dash of yellow in an email might be right up her street and just the tonic to turn a frown upside down on a windy day.

Why does being professional have to mean being incredibly serious and scary? We're all human and being kind is our nature. Business is sometimes serious because a job has to get done well, but maybe it's time we learned to achieve the same results with a splash of kindness on life's canvas.

9

Kindness conundrums

Mark Twain said that kindness is the language that the deaf can hear and the blind can see. It's something that transcends borders, cultures, and ages.

And, for the most part, that's completely true. As we know, being kind can bring a smile to someone's face, make a day brighter, or even change a life. Yet, as simple as the notion of 'being kind' sounds, sometimes the world throws situations at us where the kindest choice isn't crystal clear.

I'm sure we've all known loads of times where the 'right' thing to say or do wasn't obvious. Maybe where being kind to one person got someone else's back up, because it seemed you weren't being kind to them instead. Or think about a parent disciplining their child. The immediate 'kind' thing might seem to let the child have their way. But if that means letting them touch a hot cooker, the immediate kindness can lead to harm.

Sometimes, kindness might look like tough love or setting boundaries. It's like teaching someone to fish instead of just giving them a haddock; the former ensures they're fed for a lifetime. Which one is the kinder act depends on how we look at it. Or consider when a friend is engaging in harmful behavior. The easy, 'kind' thing might be to avoid confrontation and let them continue, hoping that they might stop. But the true act of kindness could be the difficult conversation that might risk the friendship but saves the friend.

There's rarely a one-size-fits-all answer to what kindness looks like in every situation. Our world is filled with complexities, and sometimes what feels kind to you might not be in the best interest of the person or situation at hand. There are times when being honest could potentially hurt someone's feelings, damage a fragile self-esteem, or make a dent in a person's mental health. And other times, when what seems harsh might be the kindest thing you can do in the long run.

The trick is to approach situations with empathy, understanding, and patience. Ask yourself: 'Am I acting out of love, concern, and genuine care?' If the answer is yes, then even if the path isn't clear, your intentions are rooted in the right place. And that in itself is a form of kindness.

Forms of kindness can be as diverse and multifaceted as the situations we find ourselves in. I've noticed that if we try to keep an open heart, the right sort of kindness eventually finds its way into the situation. In celebration of the multiple colors, tones, and notes of kindness, here's a handful of challenging questions about if and when to be kind, and other conundrums that can sometimes give us a headache.

1. Can you ever be 'too kind'?

We've all heard it: 'Kindness is cool,' 'kindness is the new black,' and 'kindness rocks.' And this is so true. I mean, who doesn't love a kind soul? But here's the curly question: Can you ever be *too* kind?

I've met loads of people who've been told that they are exactly that. It's usually in the context of a friend warning them against being walked all over. Yet it's not completely clear-cut, as it depends on the person and the situation. Some people spread kindness freely and never give a thought for any seeming drawbacks. Kind is who they are. It's just their nature and they won't be drawn into debates. Kindness is like confetti to them, and they sprinkle it freely.

An old friend of mine has such a light, kind spirit. She once told me she refuses to let other people's unkindness change who she is. Some call her naive. She considers them cynical. She trusts that, in time, her spirit will attract to her only those people who appreciate her for who she is. She realizes that there are those who'll take advantage of her good nature, but she says you can usually tell – and she's learned where to draw the line on occasion. We learn from experience, after all. But we needn't let other people's behavior change us.

Personally, I think the world could do with more people like my friend. Their kindness is unconditional. It's warm. It's genuine.

Yes, sometimes we may get drawn into other people's lives and needs too much, but it's about learning to recognize when we need to practice self-kindness and say 'no.' That's a skill in life: finding some middle ground. Because it is possible to help too much. Years ago, another friend of mine went into debt after repeatedly helping someone financially.

Here's another reason why you may sometimes need to aim your confetti with a bit more discretion. Maybe you're always there for a friend, lending a hand whenever they need it. But if you're *always* catching them before they stumble, it's like never letting a toddler fall as part of learning to walk. Sometimes, we have to let people face a bit of the music they're making: It helps them get into their own groove.

So, can you be too kind? Kindness is totally the right thing to do, but there's a fine line between being a superhero and spreading yourself too thin. And that line falls in a different place for each of us. What's right for one isn't necessarily right for another. It's about finding that sweet spot we talked about earlier – for our own health. Be awesome, be kind, be brave, but also make sure you're looking after yourself!

2. Can kindness be manipulative?

We get that kindness can be as comforting as a cup of hot cocoa on a chilly evening. And we usually think of kind gestures as the embodiment of pure intentions, like helping an elderly neighbor, looking after a friend's cat, or letting someone know there's a label sticking out the back of their shirt. So here's the puzzler: Can kindness, in some instances, have an ulterior motive?

Now, before anyone gets riled up, let's clear the air: I'm not saying kindness is *inherently* sneaky or deceitful, or that you, personally, ever have an ulterior motive. But I know some people believe there's always strings attached, so that's why I'm including this question. I mean, we usually benefit from acts of kindness – psychologically and physiologically – and this is because, as we know, we're wired to benefit from it; it's in our DNA, Nature's reward for good behavior. The thing is, knowing that we benefit from it doesn't mean this is *why* we're being kind. You can still be kind because you're moved to help someone. Most kind intentions are clean, in my opinion.

Then again, just as a chef can use sugar both to sweeten a pie or to mask an overly salty broth, kindness can be genuine and sometimes it can be, well, a bit strategic. Telling the difference comes with experience and intuition. Here are some thoughts on this.

Genuine kindness versus kindness with a catch

Strategic kindness is when someone uses kind gestures with an end goal in mind, apart from the pure joy of being nice. Strategic kindness is a bit like making an investment: There's an expected return. For example, maybe you know someone who's always quick to offer a favor, but somehow there's always a string attached.

Or perhaps there's that co-worker who brings in pastries every Monday but always ends up subtly mentioning those pastries when tasks are being delegated, or during promotion season. Maybe they deserve that promotion, but maybe they're swaying favor away from someone who deserves it more.... Then again, maybe the co-worker wants to bring in pastries because that's the sort of genuinely kind thing they do. In which case, should they refrain from being kind in case it's misconstrued?

My experience is that you can usually tell genuine kindness. There's a warmth to it. It's often spontaneous, selfless, and doesn't expect anything in return. It's that person who helps you pick up your scattered papers without hoping for a thank-you coffee later on.

Navigating the world of niceness

It can feel like a minefield when you start wondering if every nice gesture comes with an asterisk. I say this because we all find ourselves in different environments. Some of us may be surrounded by genuine kindness all the time, but some aren't. Intuition is often our greatest asset when it comes to knowing the difference.

With certain people, we can just tell they're doing a good thing, or at least trying to work on being kinder, so let's cut them some slack. With those where kind acts are quite plainly strategic, take them with a pinch of salt. Register the kindness, but be on the lookout for the strings attached. Learn to say no if you think it might cost you in the long run, whether in terms of your time or even your sanity.

Here's the kicker: Depending on how we look at it, it's OK to be both genuine and strategic with our kindness. After all, we all have agendas, goals, and desires, and there's nothing *inherently* wrong with aligning some of our good deeds with those objectives. However, it's the transparency and sincerity behind those actions that matter most. If you're always expecting payback for your good deeds, you might be veering into manipulative territory.

The key is to be kind and genuinely mean it. Put the kindness first. It's OK to know in the background that this might also serve your goals, but be kind *in the moment* because it's the right thing. Let the cards land as they will; let any benefits happen by themselves.

The takeaway from all this is that while kindness can be really straightforward, it's not always as simple as it seems. But while it's true that kindness can be used as a tool for manipulation, let's not forget the countless instances when it's just pure, selfless love. Don't let some manipulative behavior make you think that everyone behaves like that. As with many things in life, it's all about balance and authenticity.

So, next time someone offers you an unexpected coffee or holds the door open a little longer than usual, take a moment to appreciate the gesture. But also, maybe, keep an eye out for those pastries come promotion season!

3. Is it OK to cause pain if it serves a greater good?

First off, how many times have we heard 'It's for your own good!' while enduring something quite unpleasant? Maybe it was when your friend dragged you to that super-intense spin class or when you took that horrible medicine. Argh! But now you're grateful that you're healthier or, you know, not catching a disease.

Then there's the whole concept of 'tough love' – like the teacher who refuses to accept yet another late assignment because she wants to teach her student about accountability and time management. Or when parents won't buy their teenager a new smartphone after he's broken it for the second time, as they want to teach him responsibility. It's not about being mean, but about fostering growth, responsibility, and independence.

On a larger scale, societies sometimes implement policies that might hurt a few but are believed to benefit the majority. Think about taxes. Nobody jumps with joy at the thought of parting with their hard-earned money, but then we appreciate the roads, schools, and public services those taxes fund. And businesses sometimes have to make some redundancies in order to keep going so that others can still feed their children.

Hold on a sec, though. Just because something *seems* like it serves a greater good doesn't make it ethically A-OK. There's a bit of moral math we have to do. One person's 'greater good' might be another's 'unthinkable act.' And context, as they say, is everything. It depends on the situation. So while there's no one-size-fits-all answer, it's essential to approach these kinds of decisions with compassion, reflection, and a generous dollop of moral nuance.

What really matters is the intention behind the pain or discomfort, and ensuring it truly is for a greater good. Because, let's be honest, nobody likes unnecessary suffering. As Spider-Man's Uncle Ben wisely put it: 'With great power comes great responsibility.' When in a position to cause pain, even for a greater purpose, it's essential to handle the situation with empathy, understanding, and a clear vision of the long-term goal. While a little temporary pain can sometimes lead to great things (like better immunity or life lessons), it's vital to ensure that the scales tip toward genuine benefits and not just short-term conveniences or misguided intentions. And always, always make sure to have a soothing Band-Aid or comforting hug at the ready.

So, next time your friend tries to pull you into that spin class with the 'greater good' argument, you can fire back with some philosophical ponderings. Who knows, you might just get out of leg day!

4. Should kindness be indiscriminate?

A number of years ago, while on a trip in South America, my friends and I noted that there were several children begging on the streets or selling small wares. Some had mutilations to their limbs. I was about to give some money to a little girl, but my friend smacked my hand. He'd traveled a lot and was quite worldly wise. He told me that criminal gangs force children onto the streets to beg. Tourists feel sorry for them and give them money. He said that the more money the children are given, the more it drives the gangs to continue the exploitation.

I was torn. I didn't want to enable such gangs. But maybe the little girl was genuinely poverty-stricken and in need of money for her family.... How could I know? The answer is that, in life, we can't always know for sure. This is true of a lot of things, just as we can't know what someone else is going through.

In which case, should we sprinkle our kindness indiscriminately, like confetti at a party, or should we be a bit more selective? Some argue that kindness should come with discernment. After all, in a world where resources (including emotional ones) are finite, maybe we should channel our goodwill to those who truly deserve it – to the ones who show gratitude or, perhaps, to those who are kind in return. It's a bit like investing: You wouldn't put your money into stocks that don't yield returns.

On the flip side, there's the 'kindness for all' camp. Kindness, in this view, isn't a currency to be traded, but a universal energy to be shared. It's like sunlight: It doesn't pick and choose where to shine; it just does. It's like that friend I mentioned earlier, who wouldn't allow other people's unkind behavior to change who she is.

The idea here is that the very act of being kind elevates us, irrespective of the recipient's response. And it adds kindness energy to the collective consciousness, like adding a much-needed touch of pink to an otherwise dull gray cloud. It's not about anyone 'owing' us a thank you or a smile; it's about creating ripples of positivity in the universe. It's the intention that matters, the thought behind the act that counts.

But let's add some real-world practicality here. Despite the best will in the world, it's probably not possible to be kind to everyone all the time. You might run into people who try to take advantage of your kindness. Or you might just tire out. It's a pickle, for sure. That's why boundaries are crucial, even in the world of kindness.

Bottom line? It's a personal call. Maybe you'll lean more toward 'kindness with discernment' on some days, and 'sprinkle it everywhere' on others. What's important is being genuine in your intent and true to yourself. It's OK to protect your energy and peace, but that doesn't necessarily mean withholding basic human decency.

In the end, I gave some money to the little girl, much to the annoyance of my friend. I gave less than I originally intended as I felt there might be some truth in what he said, but then again, he could be wrong. I didn't want to deprive the child of help. So I gave the money with compassion and offered a silent prayer later that 'may the energy of my gift bring a little lightness to the world,' even if the outcome of the act itself was unclear.

In my way of thinking, if the intent is genuine, you still add those kind vibes to the energy of everything that connects us.

5. How do cultural differences impact perceptions of kindness?

On a broader note, let's talk about cultural perceptions of kindness. It's something I've noticed once or twice. For example, if you're a traveler, maybe you've held a door open for someone in one country and been met with a smile, only to do the same in another and receive a puzzled look. Welcome to the delightful maze that is understanding kindness across different cultures!

Imagine this: You're in Japan and you see someone struggling with their bags. Your inner superhero urges you to swoop in and lend a hand. But wait! In Japan, drawing attention or potentially making someone feel indebted to you might not be seen in the light you'd hope. Offering assistance could make them feel embarrassed. Oops!

Now, hop on a virtual plane to Ukraine. Someone gives you a hearty pat on the back as a congratulatory gesture. If you're from a culture where personal space is sacred, you might jump a foot in the air. But in many parts of Ukraine, this is a common gesture of affection among friends.

Oh, and while we're globe-trotting, let's swing by the Middle East. Over there, it's a grand gesture of respect to offer guests a cup of tea or coffee. Declining that drink could be seen as impolite. But if you're from a culture where 'no means no,' turning down an offer is just being honest about your preferences. And then there's the art of gift-giving. While presenting a bottle of wine when visiting someone's house might be a common courtesy in France, in some Muslim-majority countries, where alcohol is forbidden, it would be a major faux pas.

It's intriguing how the same gesture can zigzag between being kind, neutral, or even rude depending on where you are in the world. It's like each culture has its own secret handshake, and the code is constantly changing!

The trick to navigating these cultural waters is to do some research into a culture before you travel. Be observant, ask questions when unsure, and approach with an open heart and mind. Remember, everyone's trying their best based on what they know. And, hey, if all else fails, a genuine smile is pretty universal. If you're the one on the receiving end of the actions of a confused traveler, be kind and trust that their heart is probably in the right place.

6. How do we balance kindness with justice?

This is a bit of a conundrum. Imagine you're having guests over and someone spills red wine on your brand-new rug. (I spilled some red wine on a friend's sofa once, but thought I'd go for the rug analogy as it might still be a raw nerve.) Oops! Your inner teapot starts steaming. On one hand, you've got the kind-hearted, teddy-bear voice whispering, 'It's OK, accidents happen!' On the other, there's the stern, judge-like voice demanding through your forced smile, 'This rug cost a fortune! Be more careful!'

OK, this scenario might seem a bit trivial, but it paints the broader picture of how we grapple with kindness and justice daily. When someone does something wrong, especially if it's serious, how do we decide between turning the other cheek and raising the gavel? Here are a few perspectives:

Kindness: the warm hug approach

Being kind often means giving people a second chance, understanding their perspective, and offering compassion, even when they've made a mistake. Accidents happen, after all, and we'd be mortified if the shoe was on the other foot. And it's about making a conscious effort to put relationships above possessions. That's what I learned as a child when a visitor accidentally damaged something in our house.

Forgiveness can be therapeutic, even when it's just a mini-forgiveness. Holding on to resentment can weigh us down like carrying a backpack full of bricks. Let's face it, none of us are perfect; who hasn't wished for a little kindness when they've messed up?

Justice: the fair play referee

Now, let's not forget our friend Justice. Justice aims to ensure fairness and accountability. If everyone just went around spilling red wine and there were no consequences, we'd have a world full of stained rugs (and sofas) and frustrated wine-drinkers. Justice says, 'Hey, you made a mess – at least help clean it up!' It's not always about punishment; sometimes it's about accepting responsibility.

Striking a balance: kind justice or just kindness?

Here's where it gets tricky. When someone commits a grave mistake, the stakes can be much higher than a ruined rug. Then it's not always as simple as forgiving and forgetting. Because sometimes the harm can't be undone, and the memories can't be erased. Showing kindness to someone who committed a wrong can take away from the kindness needed for the person harmed.

Perhaps the real question is whether we can find a middle ground, and if that depends on the circumstances. Maybe it's about holding someone accountable while still extending empathy. Think 'restorative justice,' where the focus is on healing and making amends rather than simply doling out punishments. Or consider the age-old wisdom of treating others as we'd like to be treated, which marries kindness and fairness. The thing to remember is that life's complexities often don't come with straightforward answers, but they sure do make for good conversation starters at your next dinner party (with or without the wine spiller!).

In the end, balancing kindness with justice is a personal journey, and there's no one-size-fits-all answer. But one thing's for sure: If we can master that balance, we're one step closer to hosting a dinner party where everyone feels both safe and loved. Now, who's up for a glass of wine?

7. Being kind vs. changing the world: Do we really have to choose?

Ah, kindness. It's like the comfy cardigan of human behaviors. We're often taught from a young age: 'If you can't say something nice, don't say anything at all.' But if we're constantly zipped up in our 'be-nice cardigans,' perhaps we're missing the bigger picture.... Does a perpetual focus on personal kindness put the brakes on confronting societal injustices?

Here's a scenario: You're at a family gathering and Uncle Bob, one of your favorite people, drops a casually prejudiced comment. Do you challenge it, potentially causing a scene, or pass him another slice of pie with a smile, inadvertently endorsing his harmful beliefs?

Let's be clear: Personal kindness isn't the enemy here. Small acts of compassion make day-to-day life more pleasant and can create ripple effects of positivity. Holding doors open, paying for someone's coffee, or just listening – these actions matter. They weave a web of empathy and connection in our immediate communities.

However, the crux lies in confusing kindness with complacency. If we equate 'being kind' to 'never rocking the boat,' we risk becoming silent bystanders to systemic issues. Some problems, like systemic racism or gender inequality, won't budge with a polite nudge; they require collective, sustained pushback. So where does that leave us? Must we shed our cardigans of kindness to bring about societal change?

Not necessarily. The magic lies in our old friend 'balance' again. Challenge systemic issues, but remember that every movement is made up of individuals. Sometimes, changing a single heart, when done with patience, understanding, and compassion, can ripple out to influence an entire community.

One solution in our earlier scenario could be to pass the pie but then have a quiet (and kind) word with Uncle Bob later. Explain the harm in his comment and talk to him about how best to communicate in future. It's entirely possible to be a beacon of personal kindness while advocating for systemic change. The key is not to let our desire for immediate harmony overshadow the need for long-term justice. Remember, a truly kind world is also a fair one.

8. What do you do when someone isn't being kind to you?

First things first: When someone's throwing shade your way, it's usually about them, not you. We've all got our baggage, and sometimes that suitcase opens up and clothes spill out all over the place – you just happen to be standing there when it happens. So, try not to take it to heart. It's not about you; it's their stuff.

Secondly, remember that everybody's got a story. They could be dealing with a whole circus of issues you know nothing about. Keeping this in mind helps you stay cool and compassionate, even when they're acting out.

Now, can you respond to unkindness with kindness? Well, it depends on the situation. Responding with kindness isn't about letting people walk all over you; it's about not adding fuel to the fire. You can stand your ground and still be the bigger person. Sometimes, a little kindness can turn the whole situation around. Who knows, you might just be the highlight of their day!

If the air isn't too frosty, try to talk things through. Listening and trying to understand the other person's point of view can work wonders. It's amazing how a simple 'I get where you're coming from' can make someone's walls come down. Empathy is your best friend here. Try to see the world through the other person's eyes, even if their behavior isn't the best. Understanding doesn't mean agreeing, but it can help you respond with a little more gentleness.

Now, having said all this, being kind when someone's being a bit of a grump doesn't mean you should forget to be kind to yourself. If you need to, set up those boundaries! As I said earlier, you can't pour from an empty cup and all that jazz.

And although I'm all for trying to be understanding first, sometimes the best move is not to play the game. If you're dealing with a no-win situation, or repetitive unkind behavior, it might be time to gracefully bow out. It's your prerogative. Save your energy for the battles worth fighting, with people who appreciate your awesome kindness.

At the end of the day, you never know how your response to unkindness might change a person's behavior or cause an unexpected ripple effect. You know what they say about being the change you wish to see in the world – well, it can start with how you respond to unkindness. Your kindness could be contagious, inspiring others to spread a little love in their corner of the world.

9. How do we prioritize acts of kindness?

The kindness quandary: Where to spread the love? This is a question that loads of us have. Maybe you've got a heart the size of a hot air balloon, but sometimes your pocket, your energy, and your available time feel more like they're thimble-sized. How do you juggle it all and decide where to sprinkle your kindness confetti?

The inner circle first

Because we're born with an inbuilt hierarchy of rules, it's only natural to want to focus on those closest to us first. Think of your energy like a ripple in a pond and start at the center, with your immediate family, your fur babies (pets), and your dearest friends. After all, these are the ones you'll be watching movies with on a lazy Sunday or who you'll call when you get stuck in the rain without an umbrella (well, you probably won't call your dog, but you know what I mean).

Passion-pull

Sometimes we're drawn to causes or people because of our own experiences. If you survived an illness or lost a family member to one, you're more likely to donate or volunteer in that area. Or maybe you just have a massive soft spot for baby sloths – who doesn't? Go where your heart tugs you. And if a friend is campaigning for a different cause, be honest. I'm sure they'll understand.

The 'opportunity knocks' method

Kindness doesn't always need an appointment. There's something to be said about spontaneous acts like assisting a stranger with their groceries, helping a mother carry her pram up some stairs, or just giving a compliment. These unplanned moments can sometimes be the most rewarding. Rather than spreading our energy thin, these acts tend to energize us, especially when we see what it means to the people we help. I believe that the universe has a sneaky way of putting opportunities in front of us that are important for us, and often for the purpose of developing our experience of kindness.

The capacity check

Before diving headfirst into any act of kindness, do a quick gut check. Do you have the time? The energy? The funds? It's noble to want to help, but not at the expense of burning yourself out. Remember, you can't pour from an empty cup.

Small acts, big impact

Don't underestimate the power of little deeds. Sometimes a smile, a text, or a homemade biscuit can make someone's day. Kindness doesn't have to be grand to be impactful.

In the end, choosing where and how to be kind might feel a bit like picking your favorite ice cream in a shop with a hundred options. It can be overwhelming, but here's the key point: There's no wrong choice. Whether you're going for the classic vanilla act of kindness or the unicorn sprinkle surprise, it's the intent and love behind it that counts. So, go out, be you, and spread kindness like it's glitter... just, you know, the biodegradable variety. We need to be kind to the Earth too.

10. Is kindness a responsibility or a choice?

Have you ever held the door for someone and wondered, 'Did I do that because I felt like it, or because it's just sort of socially expected?' Welcome to the age-old debate: Is kindness a responsibility or a choice?

On one hand, we have Team Responsibility. This camp believes we should be kind because it's our moral duty. After all, if everyone went around being rude or indifferent, the world would resemble a never-ending family reunion gone wrong. Team Responsibility says, 'It's not just about feeling warm and fuzzy inside. It's about creating a world where we all want to live.'

Then there's Team Choice. They argue that being kind should always come from the heart, not from some sense of obligation. To them, kindness without genuine feeling is like gifting someone a present for their birthday that's practical, but not particularly heartfelt. They say, 'If I'm going to be kind, it's because I *want* to, not because I *have* to.'

For the record, some research suggests that people get more benefit when they choose to be kind rather than if it feels like a requirement. And Nature would probably agree. As we know, Nature's catch-22 says you need to mean it to feel it, and only by feeling it do you get the positive side effects. But then again, regardless of whether you mean it, the person receiving that kindness still benefits.

So where does this leave us? Perhaps it's a bit of both. Sometimes, our moral compass tells us to be kind even when we're not feeling up to it. Other times, we're moved by pure, spontaneous generosity. And sometimes, you do a kindness because you feel it's the right thing to do, but at the same time you're 100 percent choosing it.

Whether it's a responsibility, a choice, or a bit of both, one thing is clear: Kindness makes the world go round. Whether you're dishing it out because you believe it's your duty or simply because you're feeling generous, I say keep spreading the love. The world can always use it!

11. Does the intent behind kindness matter?

I self-published my first book, *It's the Thought that Counts*, back in 2005. It's mostly about the mind-body connection, but the title is something my mum always said when I was a child. She meant that it's not always what you do that matters, but the thought behind it. The intent. While Nature's catch-22 means that genuine intent matters if you're the giver, does it matter quite so much if you're on the receiving end?

Let's imagine you're having one of those 'ugh' kind of days, and a stranger offers you their seat on a packed underground train. Most of us would feel grateful. Now, imagine that the stranger only offered you that seat to impress someone they're with. Would that make the seat any less comfortable or your day any less brightened?

Here's the thing: Acts of kindness, regardless of the intent behind them, often result in good outcomes. A warm smile, a small gesture, or a considerate action can flip someone's day around. The *receiver* of kindness doesn't necessarily care about the intent of the doer, as long as they benefit from the kindness.

However, from the giver's perspective, intent can be more complex. Acts of kindness with ulterior motives might score points in the short run (hey, who doesn't want to look good in front of their crush?), but in the long run, people can usually sniff out insincerity. And then there's our old friend Nature's catch-22 that I mentioned a moment ago. If you don't mean it, you won't feel it, so no kindness hormones for you.

That said, there's also a heartwarming silver lining. Even if someone starts off performing kind acts for less than pure reasons, the positive feedback from those acts might just nudge them onto the path of genuine kindness. After all, when you see the difference you make in someone's day, it's hard not to get addicted to those happy hormones and the feel-good buzz.

In a nutshell, the outcome of kindness is undeniably valuable. As for pure intent – that's the secret ingredient for sustained heart-to-heart connections.

12. Does reciprocity matter in kindness?

This is a topic we've all probably mulled over a time or two: reciprocity in kindness. You know, that little niggling thought at the back of our minds when we do something nice, wondering, 'Hmm, will they return the favor?'

Let's just put it out there: It feels good when someone returns our kindness. Maybe it's a simple nod of thanks when you hold the door, or perhaps a friend treating you to your favorite pastry just because you did the same last week. That reciprocity can be a little pat on the back, whispering, 'You did good, and someone noticed!' But here's where the rubber meets the road: Should we actually *expect* kindness in return?

On one hand, we live in a society where 'you scratch my back, I'll scratch yours' is a deeply rooted norm. A little return on kindness can be a reinforcement, encouraging more and more good deeds. It's like when we were kids: Do your chores and get an allowance. Good behavior gets rewarded.

Yet if we tie our acts of kindness to expected outcomes, we might grow a wee bit disappointed. Not everyone will have the same understanding of kindness, and not everyone's in the place to reciprocate anyway. We don't know what other stuff people are juggling. They might intend to do something in return, but other constraints and commitments take over.

Some of the purest forms of kindness are those acts done away from the spotlight, without an audience, and without a ledger keeping score. It's that anonymous donation, or when somebody secretly tidies up the neighborhood. It's driving a friend or family member wherever they need to go, no matter what time it is. A doctor friend told me that a patient secretly decorates a tree outside the local surgery every Christmas and no one has ever found out who it is. When kindness is given freely, without the strings of expectation attached, it's like a gift that's its own reward.

In the grand scheme of things, it boils down to why we're being kind in the first place. If it's genuinely from the heart, then whether or not it's reciprocated doesn't change the value of the act. But if it's done in hopes of getting something back, we might need to check in with our motivations. Work on ourselves a bit.

But if do we find ourselves in one of those situations where we seem to keep on giving and giving, yet we never receive any thanks, well, that can even wear down a saint. Here, self-kindness might shout out 'Stop!' – to leave the situation, if you can, or change your part in perpetuating it, especially if it's making you feel resentful.

When it comes to kindness, reciprocity can be the cherry on top of a feel-good sundae. But the real magic is in the act of giving itself, no strings attached. Sometimes the best things in life are those done just for the joy of them. The world becomes a little brighter with each act of kindness, whether it's reciprocated or not.

Kindness isn't always clear-cut

There's a joke that Billy Connolly, the Scottish comedian and actor, once told during a live show. It's about two filmmakers in the Serengeti who are filming wildebeests. Suddenly, one of them spots a lion stalking them, ready to pounce. They both panic, sure this is the end. One of them bends down and pulls a pair of Nike trainers out of his bag. He speedily ties up the laces. The other says to him, 'What are you doing? You'll never outrun a lion.' His friend replies, 'But if I can outrun you...'.

Life isn't always so extreme, yet the basic choice is one we frequently make in gentler contexts: Help you or help me. Be kind to you or be kind to me. But there's often a third way: Help us both. Life isn't black and white. There's a whole rainbow of colors in between if we pause and really look.

Ever heard of the trolley problem? It's one of those classic philosophical conundrums that sounds as if it comes straight out of a dramatic movie. You're standing beside some trolley tracks, chilling out, enjoying the sun, and suddenly you see a runaway trolley speeding toward five people who are tied up on the tracks. Dramatic, right?

It gets even spicier! You suddenly notice you're next to a big lever, and if you pull it, the trolley will switch tracks. Phew, the five people are saved! You're a hero, give yourself a pat on the back. But here's the twist: There's another person tied up on the other track. Pulling the lever to save the five will send the trolley toward that person instead.

Now you're in a moral pickle. Do nothing and let the trolley take out the five people, or pull the lever and be the *direct cause* of one person's demise?

You might think, 'Well, surely saving five people is the logical choice!' But many people feel torn about actively causing harm to save others. It's a classic debate about what's known as utilitarianism (the greatest good for the greatest number) versus deontological ethics (the idea that some actions are inherently right or wrong, regardless of outcomes).

It's like the famous scene from *Star Trek: The Wrath of Khan* where Spock is trapped in a chamber filled with radiation that's killing him. Captain Kirk wants to save him, but if he does then he'll endanger many other lives. Spock says, 'Logic dictates that the needs of the many outweigh the needs of the few.' Utilitarianism.

Then again, what if the five people you just saved were mass murderers, hell bent on killing everyone? They were on the tracks as a last resort for everyone else's protection.

The right choice isn't always obvious. There isn't a simple rule book that says: Do this all the time and you'll be happy, everyone else will be happy, and everything will be awesome and hunky dory in your life. Oh, and you'll also wake up every morning with a smile on your face and feel like springing out of bed. The sun will be shining too. Sometimes you need to make a judgment call. Sometimes you'll get it right. Sometimes you won't. Sometimes you win. Sometimes you f*ck up. Welcome to real life.

Don't worry if you find yourself in a bit of a pickle about the trolley problem. This isn't an 'end of the book' test you must pass to check you've taken on board everything you've learned so far, so you can graduate as a kind person. There's no absolute right answer because it all depends on the context.

As decades of psychology students have come to learn, the trolley problem is less about finding the 'right' answer and more about understanding context and our own moral compass. Philosophers and psychologists have been scratching their heads and engaging in heated debates about it for years.

In case you were wondering, there are other solutions that result in nobody getting killed by the trolley. Maybe you find a sledgehammer and you're able to disable the tracks so that nobody dies. Or maybe you're able to run toward the trolley, board it, and quickly pull the brakes. Or maybe someone else intervenes and, between the two of you, you're able to evacuate everyone from the tracks. Or perhaps you sacrifice yourself by lying across the tracks.

It's not a problem if the seeming 'right' answer doesn't slap you on the face. Because just when you think you've cracked it, there's always another twist or version to consider! Same as life.

It's a handy dinner conversation subject at the very least. Next time you're with friends and want to stir the pot a bit, drop the trolley problem on them. It'll keep you going for hours.

It's about context

Let's play with the idea of context a bit, because what's 'kind' in one situation might seem, well, not so kind in another.

Take the example of a child wanting sweets. In the wee one's eyes, a cool parent would just hand the sweets over. But if the parent is thinking about avoiding sugar crashes and cavities, they might say no. Not so much being mean, but actually looking out for the child in the long run. Mean from the kid's perspective, perhaps, but kind from the parent's.

And that's the thing: our viewpoint matters. Context molds our perceptions. It's the lens through which actions are magnified, intentions are interpreted, and we form judgments.

Kindness isn't just about doing what seems good right now; it's sometimes about what's actually best for everyone involved in the long run. It's like when a friend tells you there's spinach stuck between your teeth. Sure, it's a bit awkward, but it's kinder than letting you walk around like that all day. Life's full of these weird moments, where what seems sort of 'meh' actually turns out to be super thoughtful.

My advice is next time you're about to judge, remember to check out the whole story. You never know what a person is going through, and real kindness is all about doing good even when it doesn't look or feel like it straightaway, or when nobody is looking.

It's all a question of context. In an era of black and white, and division, understanding the shades of color in between becomes imperative – and takes skill. Empathy comes in handy. It's the emotional currency that helps us better understand and relate to each other. Because amidst varying contexts, there is a common thread: Genuine kindness always *seeks* the highest good, even when that isn't immediately apparent. Through kindness, as the author and poet Khalil Gibran might say, the heart finds its morning and is refreshed.

My simple prayer is that as we each navigate our way through the labyrinth of life, may we be equipped with the wisdom to discern the contexts and, with it, the true nature of kindness. Because while kindness might wear different masks, its heart remains unchanged: a genuine desire for the well-being of others.

Contextual ethics

The above quandaries, where the answer isn't immediately clear, fit into what's more broadly known as contextual ethics. It's like when you run into a situation where you're wondering, 'Is this the right thing to do?' and someone chimes in with, 'Well, it depends...' when all you want is a straight answer. Welcome to the world of contextual (or situational) ethics! Basically, it's the idea that the right move might change, depending on the situation.

In *Les Misérables,* Jean Valjean was locked up for 19 years for stealing a loaf of bread (five years for the bread and the rest for attempts to escape). But his need was urgent. His sister's son was terribly sick and nearing death. They were starving. He based his actions upon the idea that the shop owner had an abundance and might not miss one loaf of bread. Yet his punishment was based in the concept of absolute right and wrong, which a set of laws were built around.

Almost anything can be considered from a different viewpoint. Thou shalt not kill. Respect all life. But what about on the battlefield, when stopping an attacker might save millions of lives? In the ethical discussions on mindfulness in academia, some scholars have criticized the teaching of mindfulness to the military. They believe it betrays the ethics of Buddhism and the core principle of non-harming.

You see, while mindfulness might help soldiers be more relaxed and improve their concentration and even their mental health – and surely they have a right to know the practice if it can help them – suppose a sniper's concentration is improved so much from mindfulness that he shoots and kills someone. But here's the thing: That sniper's decision to shoot or not comes out of weighing up different contingencies. The sniper might shoot someone, but the person who was shot might have gone on to kill several members of the sniper's own side.... It's a tricky balance: Yes, respect all life, but isn't saving multiple lives a consideration too?

Life is full of pickles, though they're usually not so much about saving or taking lives, but the small stuff – like which of your relatives' homes to visit for Christmas when they've all extended an invitation, or who to promote: the loyal colleague or the newbie who is much better at the job. You want to be kind to everyone.

Contextual ethics is like real life, only we don't go around calling it by that name; we'd all sound like stuffy academics. But sometimes life does feels like we're sitting an exam and we're not allowed a calculator. Sometimes it's straightforward because the context is clear and agreed by all. Sometimes it's not. Instead of following a rule book, contextual ethics says, 'Let's look at what's happening right now and figure out what's right or wrong based on the situation.'

Let me offer another *Star Trek* example. I'm a fan! You've probably noticed. Think of the 'prime directive.' It's the number one rule and it relates to non-interference in the development of a culture. Yet every captain has bent it, because sometimes it's meant saving lives.

The cool thing about the contextual ethics approach is that it's flexible. It's less about strict 'dos' and 'don'ts,' and more about navigating the gray areas. That's where the fun in life lies. But that doesn't mean anything goes. While contextual ethics can be flexible, it's crucial to have a strong foundation. Kindness, respect, understanding – these are the roots that guide us. Without these foundations, we risk drifting into 'anything's OK if the situation says so,' which isn't quite so cool.

Next time you're facing a tough choice, remember: It's not always black and white. Dive deep, look at the context, and aim to make decisions with a heart and mind full of kindness and understanding.

Two basic principles for living harmoniously on planet Earth

In *Beyond Religion: Ethics for a Whole World*, H.H. the Dalai Lama suggests there are two basic principles upon which we could build a universal set of ethics and guidelines that transcend religion, and that we can grasp them based on our common experience. It's like a basic universal playbook for how to navigate life; a North Star for all of us. The principles are simple, profound, and universal:

1. Our shared humanity and pursuit of happiness.

2. Our interdependence.

Let me shed a wee bit of light on them.

Our shared humanity and pursuit of happiness

First things first: We're all human. Shocking, I know! And despite the myriad of ways we express our humanness – through culture, language, cuisine, dance, and so on – deep down, we all share some common goals. Whether you're sipping tea in England or dancing to salsa beats in Colombia, chances are you're doing it in pursuit of happiness, comfort, or joy.

It doesn't matter where you're from or what language you speak; that warm, fuzzy feeling of happiness is universal. Recognizing this shared emotion means understanding that the person next to you, or halfway across the world, essentially wants the same thing as you do: a good, happy life.

Next time you find it hard to relate to someone else, just remember: Deep down, they're chasing the same joy and contentment as you, even if it doesn't seem so on the surface. And that's a beautiful thing to know.

Our beautiful web of interdependence

OK, onto our second big idea: interdependence. Now, I'm not just talking about how your morning coffee depends on a farmer from another continent (though that's totally valid). No, it's even bigger than that.

We live in a world where everything is interconnected. The air you breathe, the food on your plate, the technology you use – all the result of a collaborative dance between nature and human effort. The choices we make affect others, often in ways we may not see. In return, we're influenced by countless invisible threads that connect us to people, animals, and the environment.

Realizing our interdependence means understanding that when we help others, we help ourselves. And when we harm others, it might just come back to bite us. It means realizing that actions have consequences far wider than we initially expect.

In short, if we can hold onto these two basic ideas – our shared quest for happiness and our interdependence – we'll be well on our way to having happier households, neighborhoods, communities, and – heck, let's go all out here – a happier and kinder world too.

Let's cherish our similarities, celebrate our differences, and always remember: We're in this together! Despite appearances, despite what people say, the language they use, the image they attempt to project, we all share the same basic struggles. These struggles merely show up in different forms, with different hats on, and with different players in each game. But it's the same play, the same dance. It's life and it's being human.

No matter who you meet or interact with – rich or poor, middle class or homeless, black, white, brown, tall, short, well-dressed or in tatters – that person is a human being just like you and, despite appearances, is seeking the same basic things that you do. To be happy. To feel at peace. To avoid pain and suffering.

The things that seem to sit between us and divide us are more superficial that we realize. Where there are differences, let's celebrate them. The things we share, on the other hand, are innate to all of us. For example, a mother has a maternal instinct that's innate. It's what prompts her to set aside her own pain or discomfort, and often exhaustion, as she rocks her child to sleep in the middle of the night. It's got nothing to do with how many exams she passed, nor how much money she has, the clothes she wears, or even her knowledge of the benefits of being kind. It's the deep nature of virtually every mother on our planet.

Love, empathy, compassion, and kindness are innate to all of us. This shared spirit unites us. These values transcend all religions and spiritual traditions. They are taught by religions, but they are not religious values. They are human values. And they are values that we can cultivate. We can take the feelings we naturally have for those closest to us and we can learn to extend them farther afield.

There doesn't need to be a *them* or *us*. Let there be *we*.

A universal set of 'kindlines'

Given what I said about context, rather than having a stubborn set of rules to help us navigate life's gifts, let's have a go at crafting a set of guidelines for living kindly, which can help us through life's ups and downs. Let's call them kindlines. Get it? Kind guidelines. Guidelines for living kindly. Oh well, at least indulge me.

It's not about following these kindlines to the letter of the law. Instead, we can use them as a reference to check ourselves against from time to time. Like a magnetic north for our inner GPS. You might not agree with every part of them, but they're a start. So here they are:

1. Respect all life

Treat all living beings, from humans to animals, with respect and kindness, recognizing the intrinsic value of each life and its basic right to exist. Now, I know some people like to eat meat. I personally don't, and I'm not going to tell you what you should and shouldn't do. These are kindlines, not laws. But what I would say is let's try our best to be respectful toward all life. It's why I included the story earlier about not hurting a fly. This kindline is not always possible. We can only do our best. But if we aim our sights high, who knows what we might achieve together.

2. Cultivate empathy

Understand that everyone has a story. It might be different from yours, but that's what being human is about. It's part of the journey. You never know what a person is going through, so err on the side of kindness. Most people are trying their best given the knowledge they have, and the experiences and influences they've known. Place yourself in the shoes of others. Try to understand their feelings, perspectives, and needs. Let this empathy be the fuel for your actions and decisions.

3. Be helpful

Look out for people. Act on opportunities to help. Share your knowledge and time with others. Give to charity if you're able. Help those less fortunate to alleviate their suffering and promote their well-being.

4. Promote honesty and integrity

Be honest in all your dealings. Don't tell lies. Don't spread gossip or rumors. You never know what someone is going through, nor the context they're living within, nor can you predict the consequences of gossip or rumors. If you don't have anything nice to say, don't say anything at all. Do what you believe is right. Let your moral compass guide your choices and actions. Spread accurate information and encourage open, respectful discussions.

5. Encourage unity and inclusion

Celebrate the diversity of human experiences, cultures, sexual orientations. Include rather than exclude. Let your words and actions unite rather than divide so that you help bridge some of the divides that separate us at whichever scale is relevant to you – whether in your household, neighborhood, workplace, country, or globally. Try for understanding and collaboration over hostility.

6. Care for the environment

Recognize the Earth as our shared home. As best you can, adopt sustainable practices, reduce waste, and support initiatives that protect our planet and climate for future generations. It's not just about our lives today and our habitual comforts, it's about our children and our children's children. Let's behave in ways that give them a clean environment in which to build their own lives and families.

7. Continue learning

Stay curious, open-minded, and willing to learn from others and about others. This helps deepen our relationships and interconnectedness. Growth and change are natural and essential parts of the human experience. Try to embrace them. See learning as something that enhances you rather than something you have to do.

8. Prioritize your well-being

Recognize your own needs and ensure that your actions promote your own physical, mental, and emotional well-being. If you look after yourself, you'll be better able to work with all the other kindlines.

9. Practice gratitude

Be grateful even for the seemingly small blessings in life. Gratitude is like a feel-good flashlight in our minds that highlights all the good stuff that we might overlook in our busy lives. It's a gentle high five to the people who've played an important role in our lives. It also expands: The more you focus on what you're grateful for, the more you will find to be grateful for. In this way, it builds and sustains happiness.

10. Be supportive

Lift people. Don't criticize. The world needs lifters. See the best in others and you'll help bring out the best in them. Remind yourself of the good in people, even when they're at their worst. Celebrate people's strengths rather than criticize their weaknesses. Stand up for people who are being bullied or minimized.

11. Be fair

Don't knowingly take advantage of people. Do your best to ensure that you speak and behave in a way that's fair. If you know of someone being treated unfairly, do your best to speak up. Of course, people have different ideas about what is fair that are based on their beliefs. But let the genuine warmth of the human heart be your guide.

12. Be respectful

Be respectful of people's beliefs, their sexual orientation, their culture. Respect people's property. Listen. Offer your full attention. Be polite. Avoid using offensive or derogatory language. Respect people's privacy, personal space, and boundaries. Consent is key in all interactions. Be punctual. Show respect for people's schedules and commitments. Acknowledge your mistakes and apologize sincerely when you can.

There you have it. Remember that these are guidelines, not rules. They're kindlines. I'm determined to make that word stick, too. (Here's looking at you again, dictionary editors.) They're intended to inspire and guide action, rather than dictate behavior. They're about giving us a direction to move in that might just make us happier, make others happier, and help all of us paint a more colorful, vibrant, peaceful, happier, and cozier world.

You haven't failed if you don't manage to keep them up. And you don't need to follow them in order; for example, there's no need to master respecting all life before you start throwing a bit of empathy around. Think of them as a holistic set of kindlines: Each one is in some way related to and helps enhance the others.

The ripple effect

I can't finish the book without saying something about the ripple effect. All those sweet little kindnesses you've been sprinkling are like pebbles dropped in a pond. They make ripples. And over the other side of that pond, the lily pads are rising and falling. In life, those lily pads are people's smiles. More often than not, the people benefiting from your ripple effects are people you've never met, nor will ever meet.

That's because kindness spreads to what scientists call 'three degrees of separation.' Let me illustrate this with an example. An estimate of the R-number of kindness – you know, the whole reproducibility number that we're all so familiar with nowadays – is somewhere between three and five. It varies. It depends on where you live, how many people you mix with, and other stuff.

Let's use five for this example. Suppose you do something kind for someone today. Now, because of how you made that person feel, they'll probably be kind or kinder to five people over the course of the next day or so. That's what R=5 means. Those five people are at one degree of separation from you.

I think you see where I'm going with this: Each of those five people will then probably be kind or kinder to five people. And those 25 people are at two degrees of separation from you.

How far does kindness go? Yep, three degrees of separation. Just checking you're paying attention.

Each of those 25 will also probably be kind or kinder to five people. So there you have it: 125 people benefiting from a single kind thing that you did. If life was a pond, that's 125 lily pads lifted. No wonder they say things like #kindnessiscool and #kindnessisthenewblack.

Of course, these numbers aren't exact, just rough estimates. Sometimes it's five, sometimes it's more, sometimes it's less. But the point is, kindness spreads out, like a cosmic pay-it-forward that everybody secretly plays without realizing they're doing it.

We don't all need to do big things to change the world. Little things matter – a lot! They create ripples every day. If you ever wonder if you make a difference from your own little corner of the universe, I'm saying you do. Big style!

Go kindfully

As we come to the close of our journey together, I want to leave you with a simple yet important thought: Kindness is the golden thread that weaves our lives into a cozy tapestry of warmth and light. It's the gentle hand on a shoulder, the smile shared with a stranger, and the small acts that say, 'I see you, and you matter.'

Be mindfully kind. Kind on purpose. Be kindful. If you meditate, do it with heart. This is the friendly twist on mindfulness: Mindfulness asks us to listen. Kindfulness adds, 'And care.'

Kindfulness in life means doing little things intentionally with a big heart, like dishing out genuine compliments, holding doors open, giving heartfelt thanks, lending a hand to someone who's having a tough time, or just checking in on each other.

Kindfulness is a mindset – a conscious choice to spread sunshine in a world that sometimes feels cloudy. It's understanding that each one of us is a candle, capable of lighting up the dark corners of someone else's day. And remember, when you light another's candle, it doesn't diminish your own light; it makes the world a whole lot brighter.

Kindness is a rebellion against cynicism, a dance in the rain of life's challenges, the music that fills the silence between us, creating a harmony that resonates through the hearts of all we meet. As we part ways in this book but not in spirit, I encourage you to carry this essence of kindness with you.

Let it be your compass, guiding you to actions big and small that make life not just bearable but beautiful. Be the light. Don't wait for it. Embrace kindness, and watch as it transforms your world, making it a cozier, more wonderful place.

Don't hold back. Create ripples. Be a kindness crusader. And who knows what we might achieve together on this big, beautiful, floating rock that we all share and call home.

Appendix I:
The seven-day
kindness challenge

Let's have some kindness fun. This is something you can do alone, or as a family, group of friends, or in a team. The goal is to do something kind every day for seven days.

Sound too easy? OK, let's make it a bit more interesting. There are three guidelines:

1. You have to do something different each day. So if you made someone a cup of tea on Day One, or bought coffee for a friend, or donated to charity, you can do the same thing again on another day, but that act of kindness only counts the first time in this challenge. It has to be seven different things on seven different days.

2. Move out of your comfort zone at least once. By this, I mean don't just do easy stuff like make an online donation or hold a door open. Sure, do those things too. But for this challenge, try to stretch yourself at least once. For example, if doing this practice has you feeling a little self-conscious, try something that causes some interaction that will stretch you even more. Maybe let that person behind you in the queue go in front – and make the offer with a genuine smile. Or pay a compliment to someone and really mean it. Or volunteer somewhere new.

3. At least one of your acts of kindness must be anonymous. No one gets to know what you did. Even if people are aware of the kindness, don't let them know it was you.

So there you go. Have some fun, spread some kind vibes, make someone's day, raise a few smiles, and make the world a better place. Oh, and if you think of yourself as a true kindness crusader, you can do more than seven kindnesses in seven days. Go all out and try to keep it up over 21 days.

Appendix II: Kindfulness meditation practices

Here's a handful of short kindfulness practices that can help you generate a consistent daily sentiment of compassion and kindness.

Start each of the following practices in the same way: by sitting comfortably and bringing your attention to the present moment. To do this, focus on your breath, because the breath is always in the present. Back in the day, the Buddha was also known to suggest that you imagine taking your seat halfway between heaven and Earth.

Breathe in and out in a relaxed way and let your attention settle on whichever sensations are most prominent. It might be the sound of your breath, or the sensation as it goes through your nostrils, or how it causes your tummy to go in and out, or your chest to rise and fall.

Do this for a couple of minutes until you feel relaxed. Then choose any of the following practices and continue breathing.

We share the same air

~ As you breathe, acknowledge that the air you inhale and exhale is the same air that is drawn in by and feeds other living beings. Hold this idea in your mind for a few minutes.

~ Then realize that everyone shares this act of breathing as a way of being alive. Realize that the need for air is shared by other living beings.

~ Reflect on this realization for a few minutes while you breathe calmly.

What unites us

~ As you breathe in a relaxed way, notice the state of calm and contentment that accompanies this. Acknowledge that this same state of calmness and contentment is sought by everyone and by all living beings. It's something that unites us. Hold this idea in your mind for a few minutes as you breathe calmly and comfortably.

~ Realize that regardless of where we live, how much money we have, our sexual orientation, or the color of our skin, we all seek the same happiness and freedom from suffering. Hold this idea for a few minutes as you gently breathe.

~ Note that everyone else's right to happiness is just as important as your own.

~ Notice what thoughts and feelings arise as you reflect on these ideas.

Metta version 1

~ As you breathe, place a hand or both hands over the area of your heart and mentally recite: 'May I be happy, and well, and safe. And may I feel at ease.' Say this three times.

~ Now think of someone you care about and say the same thing about them, swapping 'may I' for 'may you.' And say this three times.

~ Think of another person you care about, or even someone you don't know so well. It's your choice. Say the same thing three times for this person.

~ Now think of someone you have difficulty with and say the same thing three times for that person.

~ Next, extend your circle of goodwill and compassion all the way out and wish these things for all beings. Say: 'May all beings far and wide, young and old, in every direction, be happy, well, and safe. May they be filled with the spirit of loving kindness. And may they feel at ease.' Again, say this three times.

~ Notice what thoughts and feelings arise as you think these kind thoughts and wish these kind sentiments.

As an alternative, you can add as many people as you wish in between starting with yourself and ending with all beings. This makes the practice last as long as you wish it to.

The words recited don't have to be exactly these ones. There are several variations that people use. You might enjoy the feeling of 'May you be safe and protected,' 'May you be healthy and strong,' or 'May you be truly happy.'

You can even add kind wishes. Thinking of a particular person, you can wish something for them that you feel they'd appreciate. Or even wish that something amazing happens in their life, or that they receive a financial windfall, or that someone pays them a genuine, heartfelt compliment, or that they fall in love, or know what it's like to be loved – or anything else kind that comes to mind.

Metta version 2

Not everyone is comfortable starting metta with a focus on themselves. Starting with ourselves is the traditional form, but if that feels like a pressure then a simple act of self-compassion is to free ourselves from this requirement. It might be that, in time, as we come to learn to love ourselves more, starting with ourselves becomes easier.

The reason for starting with ourselves is to acknowledge that our own health and happiness also matter and that when we look after ourselves, we're better able to assist others.

If you prefer not to start with yourself, then just begin with anyone you wish and continue the practice as above. If you feel you're able to, include yourself whenever you wish to.

Metta version 3

This version of metta imagines that the kind intentions you wish for others are reciprocated.

As you wish each person in turn some happiness, wellness, safety, freedom from suffering, strength, love, or whichever sentiments you choose, imagine each person in turn also wishing the same for you.

For example, you might imagine them saying, 'May you too be happy, and well, and safe, and may you too feel at ease.' Then you could imagine a genuine smile and look of affection on their faces as they say these words to you.

Take in their kind sentiments and good wishes and offer your thanks.

Acknowledge that it is good to receive their kindness and that you deserve it.

Notes

Chapter 1: Kindfulness

p. 6 Mindfulness as we think of it in the West... For an outline of the history of mindfulness in the West, see: Kabat-Zinn, J. (2011), 'Some reflections on the origins of MBSR, skillful means, and the trouble with maps', *Contemporary Buddhism*, 12(1): 281–306.

p. 13 Kabat-Zinn did his utmost to speak about it in ways that didn't sound 'mystical, New Age, or well, just plain flakey.'... *Ibid*.

p. 13 MBSR has helped millions of people around the world... For a summary of scientific studies on mindfulness, showing its various benefits, see: Khoury, B. et al. (2013), 'Mindfulness-based therapy: A comprehensive meta-analysis', *Clinical Psychology Review*, 33(6): 763–71; Goyal, M. et al. (2014), 'Meditation programs for psychological stress and well-being', *JAMA Internal Medicine*, 174(3): 357–68; Garland, E.L. et al. (2020), 'Mind–body therapies for opioid-treated pain', *JAMA Internal Medicine*, 180(1): 91–105; Priddy, S.E. (2018), 'Mindfulness meditation in the treatment of substance use disorders and preventing future relapse: neurocognitive mechanisms and clinical implications', *Substance Abuse and Rehabilitation*, 9: 103–14; Hölzel, B.K. et al. (2011), 'Mindfulness practice leads to increases in regional brain gray matter density', *Psychiatry Research: Neuroimaging*, 191(1): 36–43; Goldin, P. et al. (2009), 'Mindfulness meditation training and self-referential processing in social anxiety disorder: Behavioral and neural effects', *J. Cogn. Psychother.*, 23(3): 242–57.

Chapter 2: How mindfulness can make you selfish

p. 26 Researchers hooked a bunch of people up... For the study involving the girl wearing the medical moon boot, see Lim, D., Condon,

P., and DeSteno, D. (2015), 'Mindfulness and compassion: an examination of mechanism and scalability', *PlosONE*, 10(2): e0118221.

p. 29 In an experiment carried out by a different group of researchers ... For the study showing how kindness after mindfulness depended on dispositional empathy, see: Malin, Y. and Gumpel, T.P. (2022), 'Short mindfulness meditation increases help-giving intention towards a stranger in distress', *Mindfulness*, 13: 2337–46.

p. 30 Mindfulness acts like a stretching exercise... For discussion on how mindfulness stretches you in the direction of your personal values, see: Brown, K.W. and Ryan, R.M. (2003), 'The benefits of being present: Mindfulness and its role in psychological wellbeing', *J. Pers. Soc. Psychol.*, 84: 822–48.

p. 31 Mindfulness backfired among those who seemed to need it the most... Ridderinkhoff, A. et al. (2017), 'Does mindfulness meditation increase empathy?: An experiment', *Self Identity*, 16(3): 251–69.

p. 33 In 2021, Michael Poulin from the State University of New York at Buffalo did a study... Poulin M.J. et al. (2021), 'Minding your own business?: Mindfulness decreases prosocial behavior for people with independent self-construals', *Psychol. Sci.*, 32(11):1699–708.

p. 39 Yet the first thought of Raye Colbey was... Colbey, R. (2014), 'A mile in the shoes of refugees', *Sydney Morning Herald*, 21 June. Available at: https://www.smh.com.au/politics/federal/a-mile-in-the-shoes-of-refugees-20110620-1gbsa.html [Accessed: 24 November 2023]

p. 42 The researchers called it SecularM versus EthicalM... Chen, S. and Jordan, C.H. (2020), 'Incorporating ethics into brief mindfulness practice: Effects on well-being and prosocial behavior', *Mindfulness*, 11: 18–29.

Chapter 3: Superfood for your mental health

p. 50 Here's another fun fact: We have kindness genes... Carter, C.S. et al. (2020), 'Is oxytocin "nature's medicine"?', *PharmRev,* 72(4): 829–61.

p. 50 [F]our distinct reasons began to emerge... Curry, O.S. et al. (2018), 'Happy to help?: A systematic review and meta-analysis of the effects of performing acts of kindness on the well-being of the actor', *JESP*, 76: 320–329.

p. 54 Negative emotions impact the processing of color in the brain... Hamilton, D.R. (2021), Why Woo-Woo Works. London: Hay

House, Chapter 7: How perception shapes your reality. See also: Bubl, E., et al. (2010), 'Seeing gray when feeling blue?: Depression can be viewed in the eye of the diseased', *Biol. Psychiatry*, 68(2): 205–8.

p. 54 Scientists at the University of British Columbia in Canada once asked 632 people... Dunn, E.W. et al. (2008), 'Spending money on others promotes happiness', *Science*, 319: 1687–8.

p. 55 Researchers have found that giving money to charitable causes boosts happiness more... Aknin, L.B. et al. (2013), 'Making a difference matters: impact unlocks the emotional benefits of prosocial spending', *J. Econ. Behav. Organ.*, 88: 90–5.

p. 56 According to research, there are much lower rates of depression among people who regularly volunteer... Musick, M.A. et al. (2003), 'Volunteering and depression: the role of psychological and social resources in different age groups', *Soc. Sci. Med.*, 56(2): S258-64.

p. 56 In 2020, the Mental Health Foundation carried out a survey... 'Kindness and mental health', Mental Health Foundation (2020). Available at: www.mentalhealth.org.uk/explore-mental-health/kindness#:~:text=It%20helps%20reduce%20stress%2C%20brings, feelings%20of%20confidence%20and%20optimism [Accessed: 29 November 2023]

p. 56 [T]he English Quaker William Tuke declared that 'moral treatment' was a way of helping people... Hamilton, D.R. (2019), The Little Book of Kindness. London: Hay House, Chapter 2: The benefits of kindness.

p. 58 [Y]our brain releases awesome chemicals such as dopamine, serotonin, oxytocin, and natural opiates such as endorphin... Hamilton, D.R. (2018), The Five Side Effects of Kindness. London: Hay House.

p. 64 This was tested in a study of 115 highly anxious people... Trew, J.L. and Alden, L.E. (2015), 'Kindness reduces avoidance goals in socially anxious individuals', *Motiv. Emot.*, 39: 892-907.

p. 67 Some researchers at the University of British Columbia did a cool study with toddlers... Aknin, L.B., Hamlin, J.K., and Dunn, E.W. (2012), 'Giving leads to happiness in young children', *PLoS ONE*, 7(6): e39211.

p. 68 Researchers asked some kids aged between nine and 11 to do some kind deeds for a few weeks... Layous, K. et al. (2012), 'Kindness counts: prompting prosocial behavior in preadolescents boosts peer acceptance and well-being', *PLoS ONE*, 7(12): e51380.

p. 68 In one, kids watched an episode from the TV show _Lassie_... Sprafkin, J.N. Liebert, R.M., and Poulos, R.W. (1975), 'Effects of a prosocial televised example on children's helping', _J. Exp. Child Psychol._, 20(1): 119-126

p. 69 Researchers call it a 'first draft' of moral cognition... Buyukozer-Dawkins, M. et al. (2020), 'Early moral cognition: a principal-based approach', in Poeppel, D. et al. (ed.), The cognitive neurosciences (Sixth Edition). Cambridge: MIT Press.

p. 70 Psychologists at King's College London and the University of Bath did research with five- and six-year-olds... Perkins, N., Smith, P., and Chadwick, P. (2022), 'Young children's conceptualisations of kindness: a thematic analysis', _Front. Psychol._, 13: A909613.

p. 72 Volunteers in a study at Uppsala University in Sweden... Dimberg, U., Thunberg, M., and Grunedal, S. (2002), 'Facial reactions to emotional stimuli: Automatically controlled emotional responses', _Cogn. Emot._, 16(4): 449-71.

p. 73 In another experiment, volunteers were shown facial expressions... _Ibid._

Chapter 4: The opposite of stress

p. 75 There was a study where psychologists sent people a daily text asking for two scores... Raposa, E.B., Laws, H.B., and Ansell, E.B. (2015), 'Prosocial behavior mitigates the negative effects of stress in everyday life', _Clin. Psychol. Sci._, 4(4): 691-8.

p. 77 In one piece of research in this area, scientists induced a state of stress [...] But if they gave them a squirt of kindness hormone up the nose first... Petrovic, P. et al. (2008), 'Oxytocin attenuates affective evaluations of conditioned faces and amygdala activity', _J. Neurosci._, 28(26): 6607-15.

p. 78 Kindfulness activities like these can change the brain organically in a similar way to the effects of mindfulness... Lutz, A. et al. (2008), 'Regulation of the neural circuitry of emotion by compassion meditation: effects of meditative expertise', _PloS ONE_, 3(3): e1897.

p. 80 Researchers at the University of Wisconsin–Madison and Harvard Medical School once compared the brain of a Tibetan Buddhist monk... Adluru, N. et al. (2020), 'BrainAGE and regional volumetric analysis of a Buddhist monk: a longitudinal MRI case study', _Neurocase_, 26(2): 79-90.

p. 81 Another study took the aging thing a bit further and looked at the end caps on DNA... Le Nguyen, K.D. et al. (2019), 'Loving-kindness meditation slows biological aging in novices: evidence from a 12-week randomized controlled trial', *Psychoneuroendocrinology*, 108: 20-7.

p. 82 If that weren't enough, scientists did a study on skin cells... Deing, V. et al. (2013), 'Oxytocin modulates proliferation and stress responses of human skin cells: implications for atopic dermatitis', *Exp. Dermatol.*, 22(6): 399-405.

p. 83 To find out, they measured the effect of kindness on the expression of some genes relating to immune function (known as CTRA)... Nelson-Coffey, S.K. et al. (2017), 'Kindness in the blood: a randomized-controlled trial of the gene regulatory impact of prosocial behavior', *Psychoneuroendocrinology*, 81: 8-13.

p. 83 Other research asked volunteers to watch an inspiring film... McClelland, D.C. and Kirshnit, C. (1988), 'The effect of motivational arousal through films on salivary immunoglobulin A', *Psychology and Health*, 2(1): 31-52.

p. 83 Researchers decided to do a similar study with older adults... Whillans, A.V. et al. (2016), 'Is spending money on others good for your heart?', *J. Health Psychol.*, 35(6): 574-83.

p. 85 That's how kindness hormones reduce blood pressure... For the study describing how oxytocin acts as an antioxidant and an anti-inflammatory in blood vessels and immune cells, see: Szeto, A. et al. (2008), 'Oxytocin attenuates NADP-dependent superoxide activity and IL-6 secretion in macrophages and vascular cells', *Am. J. Physiol. Endocrinol. Metab.*, 295: E1495-E1501.

Chapter 5: Most heroes don't wear capes

p. 94 Brain imaging studies reveal activation in empathy regions when a person acts heroically... Zanon, M. et al. (2014), 'Brain activity and prosocial behavior in a simulated life-threatening situation', *Neuroimage*, 98: 134-46.

p. 94 Even witnessing someone in pain activates brain regions in the observer as if they themselves were in pain... Singer, T. et al. (2004), 'Empathy for pain involves the affective but not sensory components of pain', *Science*, 303(5661): 1157-62.

p. 94 The name he gave it derives from Greek and means 'swift birth.'... Magon, N. and Kalra, S. (2011), 'The orgasmic history of oxytocin: love, lust, and labor', *Indian J. Endocronol. Metab.*, 15 (Suppl. 3): S156–S161.

p. 94 [I]t participates in a wide range of other stuff too, including lactation, orgasm, social bonding, maternal behaviors, cardiovascular health… Carter, C.S. et al. (2020), 'Is oxytocin "Nature's Medicine"?', *Pharmacol. Rev.*, 72(4): 829–61.

p. 94 It is abundantly produced in response to empathy and some acts of kindness… Zak, P.J. (2015), 'Why inspiring stories make us react: the neuroscience of narrative', *Cerebrum*, 2

p. 95 [C]hanges in brain oxytocin are reflected in changes in blood oxytocin… *Ibid.*

p. 95 [I]t causes the release of nitric oxide and atrial natriuretic peptide… Gutkowska, J., Jankowski, M., and Antunes-Rodrigues, J. (2014), 'The role of oxytocin in cardiovascular regulation', *Braz. J. Med. Biol. Res.*, 47(3): 206–14.

p. 96 Researchers have now shown that giving loving emotional support to a partner or just giving someone a hug produces oxytocin… Grewen, K.M. et al. (2005), 'Effects of partner support on resting oxytocin, cortisol, norepinephrine, and blood pressure before and after warm partner contact', *Psychosom. Med.*, 67(4): 531–8.

p. 99 Oxytocin isn't just about healthy skin… Elabd, C. et al. (2014), 'Oxytocin is an age-specific circulating hormone that is necessary for muscle maintenance and regeneration', *Nat. Commun.*, 5: 4082.

p. 99 Oxytocin prohormones (substances that the body converts into hormones) kick-start the construction of heart muscle cells from embryonic stem cells… Gassanov, N. et al. (2008), 'Functional activity of the carboxyl-terminally extended oxytocin precursor peptide during cardiac differentiation of embryonic stem cells', *Stem Cells*, 26(1): 45–54.

p. 99 Then it assists in turning them into fully functional contracting heart muscle cells… Danalache, B.A. et al. (2014), 'Oxytocin-gly-lys-arg stimulates cardiomyogenesis by targeting cardiac side population cells', *Int. J. Endocrinol.*, 220(3): 277–89.

p. 100 There was a study of 17-year-olds in the AIM program which looked at their telomeres… Brody, G.H. et al. (2015), 'Prevention effects ameliorate the prospective association between nonsupportive parenting and diminishing telomere length', *Prev. Sci.*, 6(2): 171–80.

p. 102 In a study that measured the quality of interaction with a dog... Nagasawa, M. et al. (2015), 'Oxytocin-gaze positive loop and the coevolution of human–dog bonds', *Science*, 348(6232): 333-6.

p. 103 In fact, some research suggests it's as much as 400 percent lower... Friedmann, E. and Thomas, S.A. (1995), 'Pet ownership, social support, and one-year survival after acute myocardial infarction in the Cardiac Arrhythmia Suppression Trial (CAST)', *AJC*, 76: 1213-17.

p. 103 This is because large studies that look at the effects of having not only dogs, but cats or rabbits... Ogechi, I. et al. (2016), 'Pet ownership and risk of dying from cardiovascular disease among adults without major chronic medical conditions', *High Blood Press. Cardiovasc. Prev.*, 23(3): 245-53.

p. 103 Our kindness hormone is strongly correlated with the activity of the vagus nerve... Zak, P.J. (2015), 'Why inspiring stories make us react: the neuroscience of narrative', *Cerebrum*, 2.

p. 105 When we feel compassion for someone, our heart rate may decrease, and our breathing can become deeper [...] the vagus nerve powering up... Stellar, J.E. et al. (2015), 'Affective and physiological responses to the suffering of others: compassion and vagal activity', *J. Pers. Soc. Psychol.*, 108(4): 572-85.

p. 105 Some kindfulness meditation practices [...] increase vagal tone... Kok, B.E. et al. (2013), 'How positive emotions build physical health: perceived positive social connections account for the upward spiral between positive emotions and vagal tone', *Psychol. Sci.*, 24(7): 1123-32.

p. 105 [R]educe the inflammatory response to stress... Pace, T.W.W. et al. (2009), 'Effect of compassion meditation on neuroendrocrine, innate immune and behavioral responses to psychosocial stress', *Psychoneuroimmunology*, 34: 87-98.

p. 105 Kevin Tracy proposed the existence of 'the inflammatory reflex'... Tracey, K. J. (2002), 'The inflammatory reflex', *Nature*, 420(6917): 853-9

p. 106 [R]esearchers wrote that the anti-inflammatory effect of high vagus nerve activity was benefiting stage-4 patients... De Couck, M. et al. (2018), 'The role of the vagus nerve in cancer prognosis: a systematic and a comprehensive review', *J. Oncol.*, Article ID: 1236787.

Chapter 6: Mindfully kind

p. 110 A 2023 survey of 30,000 people in 16 countries... AXA (2023), 'Helping minds flourish'. Available at: https://www.axa.co.uk/about/inside-axa/helping-minds-flourish/ [Accessed: 29 November 2023]

p. 119 Patients with empathetic doctors recover faster or have better outcomes... Derksen, F. et al. (2013), 'Effectiveness of empathy in general practice: a systematic review', *Br. J. Gen. Pract.*, 63(606): e76–84.

p. 120 Research found that patients with cold symptoms recovered almost 50 percent faster... Rakel, D. et al. (2011), 'Perception of empathy in the therapeutic encounter: effects on the common cold', *Patient Education and Counseling*, 85(3): 390–7.

p. 120 And prostate cancer patients were discovered to have higher levels of key cancer-destroying cells... Yang, N. et al. (2018), 'Effects of doctors' empathy abilities on the cellular immunity of patients with advanced prostate cancer treated by orchiectomy: the mediating role of patients' stigma, self-efficacy, and anxiety,' *Patient Prefer. Adherence*, 12: 1305–14.

p. 134 What Darwin really said was that being sympathetic and working together was actually our thing... Darwin, C. (1871), The Descent of Man. London: John Murray.

Chapter 7: Why you should be kind to yourself

p. 147 In fact, researchers from the department of applied psychology and human development at the University of Toronto showed... Al-Refae, M. et al. (2021), 'A self-compassion and mindfulness-based cognitive mobile intervention (Serene) for depression, anxiety, and stress: Promoting adaptive emotional regulation and wisdom', *Front. Psychol.*, 12: Article ID: 648087.

Acknowledgments

First, I'd like to thank my partner, Elizabeth, for her unwavering support as I worked on this book. And for the numerous comments she offered that always turned out to be spot on, even if I didn't agree with them at first!

And to our dog, Daisy, whose playful and affectionate spirit has been a wonderful distraction, especially when I have been writing for hours at a time. She has a knack for knowing exactly when I need to take a break, and if I don't agree, well, she insists.

And to my mum and dad. I wouldn't be here, nor be able to do what I do, if it hadn't been for the love, kindness, and support they've given me through my whole life.

I'd like to thank the amazing editorial team I've worked with at Hay House UK – Helen Rochester and Grace Rahman – who helped steer this book from conception to print. And to all the staff at Hay House, past and present, who have helped me over the years to feel like a genuine part of the Hay House family.

Thanks to my awesome editor, Sue Lascelles, for insightful guidance and for helping to shape this book into its final form.

A big shout-out to my friend Bryce Redford, who also played an important part. His insights on writing style made a significant difference to the quality of this book and helped it evolve from being perhaps a bit on the serious side to having plenty of lighter moments sprinkled throughout.

And a big thanks to some other friends who read an early draft of the book, or some of the chapters, and gave me great feedback and advice: Angela Walker and Mary McManus for concerned and friendly advice over how often I used the f-word in the first draft; Ann Hutchison, Aimee Stewart, Maude Hirst, and Dr. Liza Thomas-Emrus for insightful comments and kind support; and Amy Polly who, as a mindfulness teacher, gave me important guidance that helped refine the first two chapters, and kindly reminded me of the difference between mindfulness meditation and mindfulness in life.

And thanks to Sam Wainwright of KIND Snacks UK for sending me a few boxes of KIND bars while I worked long hours during the last three weeks of writing.

About the Author

Dr. David R. Hamilton was formerly a scientist within the pharmaceutical industry, where he worked at developing drugs for cardiovascular disease and cancer. Inspired by the placebo effect, he left the industry to write books and educate people in how they can harness their mind and emotions to improve their health.

David is now the author of 12 books, including *How Your Mind Can Heal Your Body, The Little Book of Kindness*, and *The Five Side Effects of Kindness*. He is also a magazine columnist and a regular speaker in both the public and corporate sectors.

David is the honorary scientific advisor for 52 Lives, a charity which helps people through acts of kindness. David is an advocate for kindness and works passionately to inspire a kinder world.

www.drdavidhamilton.com

@DavidRHamiltonPhD   @DrDRHamilton

We hope you enjoyed this Hay House book. If you'd like to receive our online catalog featuring additional information on Hay House books and products, or if you'd like to find out more about the Hay Foundation, please contact:

Hay House LLC, P.O. Box 5100, Carlsbad, CA 92018-5100
(760) 431-7695 or (800) 654-5126
www.hayhouse.com® • www.hayfoundation.org

———

Published in Australia by:
Hay House Australia Publishing Pty Ltd
18/36 Ralph St., Alexandria NSW 2015
Phone: +61 (02) 9669 4299
www.hayhouse.com.au

Published in the United Kingdom by:
Hay House UK Ltd
The Sixth Floor, Watson House,
54 Baker Street, London W1U 7BU
Phone: +44 (0) 203 927 7290
www.hayhouse.co.uk

Published in India by:
Hay House Publishers (India) Pvt Ltd
Muskaan Complex, Plot No. 3,
B-2, Vasant Kunj, New Delhi 110 070
Phone: +91 11 41761620
www.hayhouse.co.in

———

**Access New Knowledge.
Anytime. Anywhere.**

Learn and evolve at your own pace
with the world's leading experts.

www.hayhouseU.com

CONNECT WITH

HAY HOUSE

ONLINE

🌐 hayhouse.co.uk   **f** @hayhouse

📷 @hayhouseuk   𝕏 @hayhouseuk

▶ @hayhouseuk   ♪ @hayhouseuk

Find out all about our latest books & card decks • Be the first to know about exclusive discounts • Interact with our authors in live broadcasts • Celebrate the cycle of the seasons with us • Watch free videos from your favourite authors • Connect with like-minded souls

'The gateways to wisdom and knowledge
are always open.'

Louise Hay